CONGRESSIONAL POLICIES, PRACTICES AND PROCEDURES

AGREEMENTS ON SOCIAL SECURITY BETWEEN THE UNITED STATES AND ICELAND, URUGUAY, AND THE REPUBLIC OF SLOVENIA

CONGRESSIONAL POLICIES, PRACTICES AND PROCEDURES

Additional books and e-books in this series can be found on Nova's website under the Series tab.

ECONOMIC ISSUES, PROBLEMS AND PERSPECTIVES

Additional books and e-books in this series can be found on Nova's website under the Series tab.

CONGRESSIONAL POLICIES, PRACTICES AND PROCEDURES

AGREEMENTS ON SOCIAL SECURITY BETWEEN THE UNITED STATES AND ICELAND, URUGUAY, AND THE REPUBLIC OF SLOVENIA

JAN KOŘÍNEK
EDITOR

Copyright © 2019 by Nova Science Publishers, Inc.

All rights reserved. No part of this book may be reproduced, stored in a retrieval system or transmitted in any form or by any means: electronic, electrostatic, magnetic, tape, mechanical photocopying, recording or otherwise without the written permission of the Publisher.

We have partnered with Copyright Clearance Center to make it easy for you to obtain permissions to reuse content from this publication. Simply navigate to this publication's page on Nova's website and locate the "Get Permission" button below the title description. This button is linked directly to the title's permission page on copyright.com. Alternatively, you can visit copyright.com and search by title, ISBN, or ISSN.

For further questions about using the service on copyright.com, please contact:
Copyright Clearance Center
Phone: +1-(978) 750-8400   Fax: +1-(978) 750-4470   E-mail: info@copyright.com.

NOTICE TO THE READER

The Publisher has taken reasonable care in the preparation of this book, but makes no expressed or implied warranty of any kind and assumes no responsibility for any errors or omissions. No liability is assumed for incidental or consequential damages in connection with or arising out of information contained in this book. The Publisher shall not be liable for any special, consequential, or exemplary damages resulting, in whole or in part, from the readers' use of, or reliance upon, this material. Any parts of this book based on government reports are so indicated and copyright is claimed for those parts to the extent applicable to compilations of such works.

Independent verification should be sought for any data, advice or recommendations contained in this book. In addition, no responsibility is assumed by the Publisher for any injury and/or damage to persons or property arising from any methods, products, instructions, ideas or otherwise contained in this publication.

This publication is designed to provide accurate and authoritative information with regard to the subject matter covered herein. It is sold with the clear understanding that the Publisher is not engaged in rendering legal or any other professional services. If legal or any other expert assistance is required, the services of a competent person should be sought. FROM A DECLARATION OF PARTICIPANTS JOINTLY ADOPTED BY A COMMITTEE OF THE AMERICAN BAR ASSOCIATION AND A COMMITTEE OF PUBLISHERS.

Additional color graphics may be available in the e-book version of this book.

Library of Congress Cataloging-in-Publication Data

ISBN: 978-1-53615-219-7

Published by Nova Science Publishers, Inc. † New York

Contents

Preface		vii
Chapter 1	Agreement on Social Security between the United States and Iceland *Message from the President of the United States*	1
Chapter 2	Agreement on Social Security between the United States and Uruguay *Message from the President of the United States*	69
Chapter 3	Agreement on Social Security between the United States and the Republic of Slovenia *Message from the President of the United States*	141
Index		213

Preface

This book contains the Agreements on Social Security between the United States and Iceland, Uruguay and the Republic of Slovenia. The Agreements are similar in objective and content to the social security totalization agreements already in force with other leading economic partners in Europe and elsewhere, including Australia, Canada, Chile, Japan, Norway, the Republic of Korea, and Switzerland. Such bilateral agreements provide for limited coordination between the United States and foreign social security systems to eliminate dual social security coverage and taxation and to help prevent the loss of benefit protection that can occur when workers divide their careers between two countries.

Chapter 1 - This is an edited, reformatted and augmented version of 115th Congress, 2d Session, Publication No. House Document 115–127, dated May 18, 2018.

Chapter 2 - This is an edited, reformatted and augmented version of 115th Congress, 2d Session, Publication No. House Document 115–102, dated March 20, 2018.

Chapter 3 - This is an edited, reformatted and augmented version of 115th Congress, 2d Session, Publication No. House Document 115–125, dated May 17, 2018.

Chapter 1

AGREEMENT ON SOCIAL SECURITY BETWEEN THE UNITED STATES AND ICELAND[*]

Message from the President of the United States

To the Congress of the United States:

Pursuant to section 233(e)(1) of the Social Security Act, as amended by the Social Security Amendments of 1977 (Public Law 95–216, 42 U.S.C. 433(e)(1)), I transmit herewith a social security totalization agreement with Iceland, titled "Agreement on Social Security between the United States of America and Iceland" and the accompanying legally binding administrative arrangement, titled "Administrative Arrangement between the Competent Authorities of the United States of America and Iceland for the Implementation of the Agreement on Social Security between the United States of America and Iceland" (collectively the

---

[*] This is an edited, reformatted and augmented version of 115th Congress, 2d Session, Publication No. House Document 115–127, dated MAY 18, 2018.

"Agreements"). The Agreements were signed at Reykjavik, Iceland, on September 27, 2016.

The Agreements are similar in objective and content to the social security totalization agreements already in force with other leading economic partners in Europe and elsewhere, including Australia, Canada, Chile, Japan, Norway, the Republic of Korea, and Switzerland. Such bilateral agreements provide for limited coordination between the United States and foreign social security systems to eliminate dual social security coverage and taxation and to help prevent the loss of benefit protection that can occur when workers divide their careers between two countries.

The Agreements contain all provisions mandated by section 233 of the Social Security Act and, pursuant to section 233(c)(4), other provisions which I deem appropriate to carry out the purposes of section 233.

I also transmit for the information of the Congress a report required by section 233(e)(1) of the Social Security Act on the estimated number of individuals who will be affected by the Agreements and the Agreements' estimated cost effect. Also included are a summary of the main provisions of the Agreements and an annotated version of the Agreements with descriptions of each article. The Department of State and the Social Security Administration concluded that these Agreements are in the national interest of the United States.

I commend to the Congress the Agreement on Social Security between the United States of America and Iceland and the Administrative Arrangement between the Competent Authorities of the United States of America and Iceland for the Implementation of the Agreement on Social Security between the United States of America and Iceland.

Donald J. Trump
The White House,
May 17, 2018.

MAIN PROVISIONS OF THE UNITED STATES (U.S.)-ICELAND SOCIAL SECURITY AGREEMENT

Introduction

In general, section 23J(c)(1) of the Social Security Act requires that international agreements concluded pursuant to that section meet three requirements.

- They must eliminate dual coverage of the same work under the social security systems of the United States and the other country that is a party to the agreement.
- They must allow for combining credits that the worker earns under the two systems for benefit eligibility purposes.
- When combined credits establish eligibility for U.S. Social Security benefits, the basis for the U.S. benefit payable must be the proportion of the worker's periods of coverage completed under title II of the Social Security Act.

The U.S.-Iceland agreement includes these required provisions.

Elimination of Dual Coverage

The agreement establishes rules to eliminate dual coverage and taxation, the situation that now exists when a person from the United States works in Iceland.

- The agreement provides that the social security system of the employee's home country will cover an employee whose employer temporarily transfers him or her from one country to work in the other country for a period of five years or less. In other cases, the country where the employee performs the work would cover the employee. Thus, a person whose U.S. employer temporarily transfers him or her to work in Iceland will retain coverage under, and pay contributions to, the U.S. program exclusively. The agreement will relieve the employer and employee of the additional burden of paying social security contributions to the Icelandic program.

- The agreement sets forth special coverage rules for employees of the governments of the two countries and for workers in international air and maritime transportation.
- The agreement also contains rules applicable to persons with earnings from self-employment who, without the agreement, would be subject to compulsory coverage under the laws of both countries. Under these rules, U.S. laws will cover a self-employed person residing in the United States, and Icelandic laws will cover a self-employed person residing in Iceland.

Totalization Benefit Provisions

In addition to eliminating dual coverage, the agreement will help prevent situations where workers suffer a loss of benefit rights because they divide their careers between the U.S. and Iceland.

- Under the rules that apply to the United States, if a person has credit for at least six quarters of coverage under the U.S. Social Security system, but not enough credits to qualify for a retirement, survivors, or disability benefit, the U.S. will totalize (i.e., combine) the person's coverage credits from both the U.S. and Iceland to determine whether the worker meets the applicable coverage requirements for retirement, survivors, or disability benefits under the U.S. Social Security system. The benefit amount payable to a person who qualifies based on totalized credits is proportional to the amount of coverage completed in the United States.

- Under the agreement, whenever Icelandic laws require periods of residence for Icelandic benefits, Iceland will add U.S. quarters of coverage to periods of Icelandic residence to determine whether a worker meets the applicable coverage requirements for retirement or disability benefits under the Icelandic social security system, provided the worker has completed at least 12 months of covered residency under the laws of Iceland. Where combined U.S. and Icelandic credits establish eligibility, Iceland will pay its ordinary flat rate benefit amount, prorated according to the total amount of years of covered residency in Iceland.

Benefit Portability

The agreement between the United States and Iceland removes restrictions that either country places on the payment of its benefits to residents of the other country. Under an exchange of diplomatic notes dating from 1980 and 1981, both countries already permit the unrestricted payment of benefits to citizens of the other country.

U.S.-ICELAND ADMINISTRATIVE ARRANGEMENT

Purpose

The administrative arrangement establishes a number of principles which serve as the basis for developing operating procedures. In particular, it authorizes the designated liaison agencies - the Social Security Administration for the United States, and the Social Insurance Administration for Iceland to develop procedures and forms necessary to implement the principal agreement.

Elimination of Dual Coverage

The administrative arrangement sets forth rules for issuing the documentation necessary to exempt workers covered under one country's system from coverage under the other country's system. These rules provide that, upon request of the worker or employer, the designated liaison agency of the country whose coverage laws apply to a person will issue a certificate of coverage that will verify the person's exemption from the other country's coverage laws.

Benefit Provisions

The U.S. Social Security Administration and the appropriate Icelandic agency will exchange coverage records and other information required to process benefit claims filed under the principal agreement. The administrative arrangement sets forth procedures governing this exchange of claims-related information.

PRINCIPAL AGREEMENT: AGREEMENT ON SOCIAL SECURITY BETWEEN THE UNITED STATES OF AMERICA AND ICELAND

The United States of America and Iceland (hereinafter referred to as the "Contracting States"), being desirous of regulating the relationship between their two countries of Social Security, have agreed as follows:

Part 1: General Provisions

Article 1: Definitions[1]

1. For the purposes of this Agreement:

---

[1] Article 1 defines key terms used in this Agreement.

(a) "national" means,
   i. as regards the United States, a national of the United States as defined in Section 101[2], Immigration and Nationality Act, as amended, and
   ii. as regards Iceland, a national of Iceland as defined in the Icelandic Nationality Act No 100/1952[3];
(b) "laws[4]" means the laws and regulations specified in Article 2 of this Agreement;
(c) "Competent Authority[5]" means,
   i. as regards the United States, the Commissioner of Social Security, and
   ii. as regards Iceland, Velferdarraduneytid (Ministry of Welfare);
(d) "agency[6]" means,
   i. as regards the United States, the Social Security Administration[7], and
   ii. as regards Iceland, for the national pension, Tryggingastofnun rikisins (Social Insurance Administration)[8], and

---

[2] Under section 10J(a)(22) of the Immigration and Nationality Act, "the term 'national of the United States' means (A) a citizen of the United States, or (B) a person who, though not a citizen of the United States, owes permanent allegiance to the United States." Those in category (B) include natives of American Samoa.

[3] The Icelandic Nationality Act No 100/1952 specifies the categories of persons to whom Iceland accords citizenship. This includes, but is not limited to, people born to at least one parent holding Icelandic citizenship at the time of birth, people who have become naturalized Icelandic citizens, and people who are able to declare Icelandic citizenship under specific circumstances. Additionally, Iceland's parliament, the Althingi, may confer citizenship on those who petition for Icelandic citizenship. Since July 1, 2003, Iceland permits dual citizenship.

[4] The term "laws," as used in this Agreement, refers to each country's social security laws and regulations as set forth in Article 2.

[5] "Competent Authority," wherever it appears in this Agreement, refers to the government official or body in each country with ultimate responsibility for administering the social security program and the provisions of this Agreement.

[6] "Agency," as used in the Agreement, refers to the administrative body in each country responsible for taking and processing claims and making coverage determinations under each country's social security laws.

[7] The Social Security Administration (SSA) is the agency for the United States. However, the U.S. Internal Revenue Service (JRS) retains its responsibility for determining Social Security tax liability based on SSA coverage determinations under this Agreement.

[8] For Iceland, the agency under its national pension system is the Social Insurance Administration (SIA). For its occupational pension scheme, the various pension funds to operate as such under Icelandic laws will serve as agencies.

iii. for the Mandatory Pension Insurance Scheme, the relevant Pension Fund;
(e) "period of coverage[9]" means,
  i. as regards the United States, a period of payment of contributions[10] or a period of earnings from employment or self-employment, as defined or recognized as a period of coverage by the laws under which such period has been completed, or any similar period insofar as it is recognized by such laws as equivalent to a period of coverage; and
  ii. as regards Iceland, residence as defined in section II of the Icelandic Social Security Act, which coincides with
    (i) periods of work or self-employment for which social security or Pension Fund contributions[11] were paid in respect of the laws specified in Article 2(1)(b) of this Agreement,
    (ii) periods before the entry into force of the Act mentioned in subparagraph (e)(i) of this Article for which a establishes that he or she worked under Icelandic laws, and
    (iii) periods for which a person establishes that he or she was self-employed under Icelandic laws;
(f) "benefit[12]" means any benefit provided for in the laws specified in Article 2 of this Agreement; and
(g) "personal data[13]" means any information relating to a specific (identified or identifiable) person, as well as any information

---

[9] "Period of coverage" means any period credited under the social security laws of either country for purposes of determining benefit eligibility, including periods of covered employment and self-employment.

[10] For the United States, this includes any contributions paid under the Federal Insurance Contributions Act (FICA), or the Self-Employment Contributions Act (SECA), as well as any periods considered equivalent to such payments under the Social Security Act (U.S. Act).

[11] For Iceland, a period of coverage includes any period for which a person made payments to a pension fund in Iceland, as well as periods prior to the establishment of the pension funds for which he or she can prove that he or she both resided and worked in Iceland.

[12] "Benefit" refers to old-age, survivors, and disability benefits provided under the social security laws of either country. With respect to the United States, the term also includes the lump-sum death payment under section 202(i) of the U.S. Act. It excludes special age-72 payments provided for certain uninsured persons under section 228 of the U.S. Act.

which can be used to distinguish or trace an individual's identity. This includes, but is not limited to, the following: any individual identifier; citizenship, nationality, statelessness or refugee status; benefits, eligibility, or other claims information; contact information; medical information or lay information used in a medical determination; information about marital, familial or personal relationships; and information pertaining to work, financial or economic status.
2. Any term not defined in this Article shall have the meaning assigned to it in the applicable laws.[14]

Article 2: Material Scope

1. For the purposes of this Agreement, the applicable laws are[15]:
   (a) as regards the United States, the laws governing the Federal old-age, survivors, and disability insurance program:
       (i) Title II of the U.S. Social Security Act and regulations pertaining thereto, except sections 226, 226A, and 228 of that title, and regulations pertaining to those sections[16], and
       (ii) Chapters 2 and 21 of the U.S. Internal Revenue Code of 1986 and regulations pertaining to those chapters[17];

---

[13] "Personal data" refers to personally identifiable information. Since there is no definition of "personal data" in the U.S. Act, this term incorporates and expands upon essential elements of the definition of "information" applying to SSA at 20 C.F.R. 401.25.

[14] If this Agreement does not define a term, that term has the same meaning as it does under each country's national laws.

[15] Article 2.1 specifies the laws to which this Agreement applies.

[16] For the United States, this Agreement applies to title II of the U.S. Act. It also applies to the corresponding tax laws (FICA and SECA) and any regulations pertaining to those Jaws. The Agreement does not apply to Medicare provisions (sections 226 and 226A of the U.S. Act). It also does not apply to provisions for special payments to uninsured individuals age 72 or over under section 228 of the U.S Act. Persons to whom this Agreement applies who qualify for Medicare hospital insurance or age-72 payments without application of this Agreement may still receive such benefits.

[17] Although this Agreement does not apply for the purposes of entitlement to Medicare, a worker who has coverage only under the Icelandic system because of Article 5 of this Agreement will be exempt from health insurance contributions under FICA and SEC. This is in

(b) as regards Iceland, the laws governing the national old-age and invalidity pension scheme[18] and the Mandatory Pension Insurance Scheme (Pension Funds)[19]:

(i) Section II and Section III of the Icelandic Social Security Act and regulations pertaining thereto, except Article 19; Article 20, paragraphs 3 and 4; and Article 18 paragraph 4, second sentence,

(ii) The Act on Mandatory Pension Insurance and on the Activities of Pension Funds and regulations pertaining thereto, except Article 15, paragraphs 2 and 3[20], and

(iii) The Icelandic Social Security Contribution Act.

2. Unless otherwise provided in this Agreement, the laws referred to in paragraph 1 of this Article shall not include treaties or other international agreements or supranational legislation on social security concluded between one Contracting State and a third

---

addition to the worker's exemption from U.S. retirement, survivors, and disability insurance contributions.

[18] For Iceland, this Agreement applies to the laws governing its first pillar residence-based benefit system, as well as the second mandatory occupational pension system. A worker subject only to U.S. laws under the coverage provisions of this Agreement or her employer will be exempt from making contributions for all mandatory Icelandic benefit and pension programs.

[19] Article 2.1 (b) excludes from the scope of this Agreement certain provisions of Icelandic law to which this Agreement will not These provisions include social assistance programs such as a supplement providing social assistance for disabled workers with low income or caring for a minor child, as well as for workers under a disability meeting certain recency-of-work requirements while residing in Iceland and contributing to an Icelandic Pension Fund (Article 19). Also excluded from the scope of this Agreement are provisions for a child benefit payable to old-age workers in special circumstances, such as prison incarceration or children of questionable paternity (paragraphs 3 and 4 of Article 20). Additionally, with respect to the invalidity benefit, a provision for calculating periods of residence in Iceland prior to a person's attainment of age 67 is not included under the scope of this Agreement (the second sentence of paragraph 4 of Article 18).

[20] The exclusion of paragraphs 2 and 3 of Article 15 of the Icelandic Act on Mandatory Pension Insurance and on the Activities of Pension Funds waives a requirement that a person must have worked recently in Iceland in order to be entitled to periodic adjustments to his or her Icelandic second pillar benefit.

State, or Jaws or regulations promulgated for their specific implementation.[21]

3. Except as provided in the following sentence, this Agreement shall also apply to legislation which amends or supplements the laws specified in paragraph 1 of this Article. This Agreement shall apply to future legislation of a Contracting State which creates new categories of beneficiaries or new benefits under the Jaws of that Contracting State unless the Competent Authority of that Contracting State notifies the Competent Authority of the other Contracting State in writing within three (3) months of the date of the official publication of the new legislation that no such extension of this Agreement is intended.[22]

Article 3: Persons Covered[23]

This Agreement shall apply to:

(a) persons who are or who have been subject to the laws of one or both Contracting States, and
(b) other persons with respect to the rights they derive from the persons described in sub-paragraph (a) of this Article.

---

[21] Except as this Agreement itself provides, the laws to which this Agreement applies do not include treaties and other international agreements. This includes either country's bilateral social agreements with third countries or multilateral agreements. This provision ensures that if a person has periods of coverage in the United States and Iceland and periods of coverage in a third country with which either country has a social security agreement, SSA cannot combine periods from all three countries to meet U.S. benefit eligibility requirements.

[22] Article 2.3 provides that this Agreement will automatically apply to any future U.S. or Icelandic legislation that amends or supplements the laws set forth in paragraph I. This includes legislation that creates new categories of beneficiaries or new benefits. The enacting the legislation may exclude it from the scope of Agreement by giving written notice to the other country within 3 months of the legislation's official publication.

[23] Article 3 specifies the persons to whom this Agreement applies. These include persons currently or previously covered under U.S. or Icelandic laws. This Agreement also applies to persons who, under the laws of either Contracting State, may derive rights by virtue of their relationship to a person subject to the laws of the United States or Iceland.

Article 4: Equality of Treatment[24]

Unless otherwise provided in this Agreement, a person designated in Article 3 of this Agreement who resides in the territory of a Contracting shall receive equal treatment with nationals of the other Contracting State in the application of the laws of the other Contracting State regarding entitlement to or payment of benefits.

Article 5: Portability of Benefits[25]

Unless otherwise provided in this Agreement, any provision of the laws of Contracting State which restricts entitlement to or payment of benefits solely because a person resides outside or is absent from the territory of State shall not be applicable to a person who resides in the territory of the other Contracting State.

---

[24] Article 4 provides that persons to whom this Agreement applies 'Nho reside in the United States or Iceland will receive the same treatment regarding benefit rights as that country gives its own nationals. The intent of this provision is to eliminate discrimination with respect to benefits based on a person's nationality. It would not affect restrictions on benefit eligibility or payment because a person is not lawfully present in that country or did not have permission to work in that country. The provision also does not affect the coverage provisions of either country's laws, since Part II of this Agreement deals with social security coverage.

[25] Article 5 provides that where the laws of either country require residence in that country in order to qualify for or receive social security benefits, a person may also qualify for and receive those benefits while residing in the other country. By virtue of an exchange of diplomatic notes in 1980 and 1981 (see Article 21.6) and SSA's published finding about Iceland's social security system (see 46 Fed. Reg. 26377), the United States currently pays benefits to Icelandic citizens who do not satisfy U.S. residency remliremenN benefit payment contained in section 202(t)(I) of However, the nonpayment exception is subject to other U.S. payment restrictions based on residency requirements for dependents and survivors; e.g., section 202(t)(ll) of the U.S. Act.

Further, both countries intend that, under this Agreement, nationals of either country may qualify for or receive benefits while residing in the other country. Accordingly, under section 233(c)(2) of the U.S. Act, this Agreement will permit the United States to pay dependents and survivors currently subject to such residency requirements as well as certain persons who are third country nationals residing in either country.

Part II: Provisions Concerning Applicable Laws[26]

Article 6: Coverage Provisions
1. Except as otherwise provided in this Article, a person employed the territory of one of the Contracting States shall, with respect to that employment, be subject to the laws of only that Contracting State.[27]
2. (a) Where a person who is normally employed in the territory of the United States by an employer in that territory is sent by that employer to the territory of Iceland for a temporary the person shall be subject to the laws of only the States as if the person were employed in the territory of the United States, provided that the period of employment in the territory of Iceland is not expected to exceed five (5) years. For purposes of applying this paragraph in the case of an employee who is sent from the territory of the United States by an employer in that to the territory of Iceland, that employer and an of the employer (as defined under the States) shall be considered one and the same, provided that the employment would have been covered under United States laws absent this Agreement.[28]

---

[26] Part II eliminates dual social security coverage, which occurs when a worker must pay social security taxes to both countries for the same earnings. The Agreement complies with the existing coverage provisions under the laws of both countries except when necessary to prevent payment of social security taxes to both countries for the same earnings. The provisions in this Part retain the worker's social security coverage and taxation in the country to whose economy he or she has the more direct connection, while exempting the worker from coverage and taxation under the other country's system.

[27] Article 6.1 establishes a basic territoriality rule, stating that ordinarily, only the country in which a person is working will compulsorily cover the worker's employment in that country. Employment that both countries would otherwise cover will remain covered exclusively under the system of the country where the worker is working. Such employment will be exempt from coverage under the other country's system.

[28] Under Article 6.2, an employee who normally works for an employer located in the United States or in Iceland who transfers to work in the other country for the same employer continue to pay social security taxes to the system of the col from which the employee transferred. This rule will apply only the employer expects the period of transfer to be 5 years or less.

(b) Where a person who is resident in the territory of Iceland and employed by an employer whose registered office or place of business is situated in that territory is sent by that employer from that territory to the territory of the United States for a temporary period, the person shall be subject to the laws of only Iceland as if the. person were employed and resident in the territory of Iceland, provided that the period of employment in the territory of the United States is not expected to exceed five (5) years.[29]

(c) If, under subparagraph (a) or (b) of this paragraph, a person continues to be subject to the laws of a Contracting State while in the territory of the other Contracting State, that subparagraph shall also apply to the person's family members who accompany the person, unless they are themselves employed or self-employed in the territory of the latter Contracting State.[30]

3. Paragraph 2 of this Article shall apply where a person who has been sent by his or her employer from the territory of a Contracting State to the territory of a third State, and who is compulsorily covered under the laws of that Contracting State while employed in the territory of the third State, is subsequently

---

[29] Article 6.2 also applies to certain workers whose United States send them to work for a subsidiary or other affiliate of that employer in Iceland. U.S. law allows American companies to extend U.S. Social Security coverage to U.S. citizens and resident aliens employed by an affiliated company in another country. To do this, the parent company in the United States must enter into an agreement with the IRS to pay Social Security contributions on behalf of all U.S. citizens and residents the foreign affiliate employs. Under Article 6.2, U.S. citizens or resident aliens an American employer sends to work for an Icelandic affiliate for 5 years or less will continue to have coverage in the United States and be exempt from. Icelandic coverage and contributions, if an IRS agreement covers the affiliate.

[30] Article 6.2 also applies to family members who accompany a worker sent from one Contracting State to the other, provided that these family members are not working in the other Contracting State. Further, in determining the length of a transfer for workers whose employer sent them from one country to the other before this Agreement entered into force, both countries will ignore any of work before this Agreement's entry into force. (See Article 21.3).

sent by that employer from the territory of the third State to the territory of the other Contracting State.[31]
4. A self-employed person who resides within the territory of a Contracting State shall be subject to the laws of only that Contracting State.[32]
5. Where the same activity is considered to be self-employment under the laws of one Contracting State and employment under the laws of the other Contracting State, that activity shall be subject to the laws of only the first Contracting State if the person is a resident of that Contracting State, and to the laws of only the other Contracting State in any other case.[33]
6. (a) A person who is employed as an officer or member of a crew on a vessel which flies the flag of one Contracting State and who would be covered under the laws of both Contracting States shall be subject to the laws of only the Contracting State whose flag the vessel flies. For purposes of the preceding sentence, a vessel which flies the flag of the United States is one defined as an American vessel under the laws of the United States.[34]

(b) Traveling employees of air transportation companies who perform work in the territories of both Contracting States and

---

[31] Under Article 6.3, the provisions of Article 6.2 will apply even if an employee did not transfer directly from one country to the other, but first transferred to work in a third country.

[32] Article 6.4 eliminates dual coverage and contributions with respect to self-employment. It provides that self-employed persons residing in Iceland will be covered only under Icelandic laws, and self-employed persons residing in the United States will be covered only under U.S. laws.

[33] Article 6.5 eliminates dual coverage in cases where a person's work activity is considered to be self-employment under the laws of one country and employment under the laws of the other and is compulsorily covered by both countries. Under Article 6.5, a who is a resident of the country which considers the work to be self-employment will be subject only to the social security laws of that country. A person who is not a resident of the country which considers the work to be self-employment will be subject to the laws of the other country.

[34] Article 6.6(a) states that an employee on a U.S. or Icelandic ship, who would otherwise have coverage in both countries, will have coverage only in the country whose flag the ship flies. U.S. law considers a ship to fly the flag of the United States if the U.S. Act defines it as an American vessel Section 210(c) of the U.S. Act defines an American vessel as one that is, "documented or numbered under the laws of the United States; and includes any vessel which is neither documented or numbered under the laws of the United States nor documented under the laws of any foreign country, if its crew is employed solely by one or more citizens or residents of the United States or corporations organized under the laws of the United States or of any State."

who would otherwise be covered under the laws of both Contracting States shall, with respect to that work, be to the laws of only the Contracting State in the of which the company has its headquarters. However, if such employees reside in the territory of the other Contracting State, they shall be subject to the laws of only that Contracting State.[35]

7. (a) This Agreement shall not affect the provisions of the Vienna Convention on Diplomatic Relations of April 18, 1961, or of the Vienna Convention on Consular Relations of April 24, 1963.[36]

(b) Nationals of one of the Contracting States who are employed by the Government of that Contracting State in the territory of the other Contracting State but who are not exempt from the laws of the other Contracting State by virtue of the Conventions mentioned in subparagraph (a) of this paragraph shall be subject to the laws of only the first Contracting State. For the purpose of this paragraph, employment by the United States Government includes employment by an instrumentality thereof, and employment by the Icelandic Government includes employment by Icelandic public employers.[37]

---

[35] Under Article 6.6(b), a member of the flight crew of an aircraft operating between the United States and Iceland who woulcl otherwise have coverage in both countries will have coverage only in the country in which the company employing the person has its headquarters. However, if the employee resides in the other country, he or she will only have coverage in that country.

[36] Article 6.7(a) specifies that the coverage provisions of this Agreement will not affect the persons to whom the Vienna Conventions on diplomatic and consular relations The Vienna Conventions, to which both the United States Iceland are parties, apply to members of the staff of a diplomatic or consular mission. This includes the diplomatic, consular, administrative, and technical staffs; family members of such staff who fonn part of their households; the domestic service staff of the mission; and private servants whom the members of such missions employ.

The Vienna Conventions usually exempt such persons from social security coverage and contributions in the host country unless specific arrangements waive their immunity from taxation. Persons whose immunity such arrangements waive would be subject to the laws of the host country and the coverage provisions of this Agreement.

[37] Under Article 6.7(b), if a U.S. or Icelandic national works for his or her country's government in the other country, but the Vienna Conventions do not apply to this person, the person will be subject only to his or her country's laws. This provision applies to U.S. Government and Icelandic Government employees, as well as to persons working for a U.S. Government instrumentality or an Icelandic public employer.

8. (a) Except as otherwise provided in this Part, a person who does not reside in the territory of Iceland shall not be subject to Icelandic laws.[38]

   (b) When a person is subject to the laws of the United States pursuant to this Article, the person and his or her employer are exempt from paying Icelandic social security contributions and contributions to a Pension Fund under the Act on Mandatory Pension Insurance and on the Activities of Pension Funds.[39]

9. The Competent Authorities of the two Contracting States may agree to grant an exception to the provisions of this Article with respect to particular persons or categories of persons, provided that any affected person shall be subject to the laws of one of the Contracting States.[40]

Part III: Provisions on Benefits[41]

Article 7: Benefits under United States Laws
The following provisions shall apply to the United States:

---

[38] Because Icelandic laws base social security contributions on residency, rather than work activity, residents who do not work may be required to contribute to the Icelandic social security programs. Article 6.8(a) makes clear that, except as otherwise provided in this Agreement (see annotations to Article 6.2(b) and (c)), only persons residing in Iceland will be subject to Icelandic laws.

[39] This provision extends the concept in Article 6.8(a) to Iceland's mandatory occupational pension scheme.

[40] Under Article 6.9, either country may grant an exception to the coverage rules of this Agreement if the other country agrees and the person involved retains coverage in one of the countries. Either country may grant such an exception to an individual worker or to all workers under similar circumstances, e.g., in the same profession or working for the same employer. This provision allows the Competent Authorities to resolve anomalous coverage situations that are unfavorable to workers or to eliminate dual coverage in unforeseen circumstances.

[41] Part III establishes the basic rules for determining social benefit entitlement when an individual has coverage in countries. It sets out the rules for determining benefit amounts when entitlement is possible only with combined work credits. Article 7 contains rules applicable to the U.S. system, and Article 8 contains rules applicable to the Icelandic system.

1. Where a person has completed at least six (6) quarters of coverage under United States laws, but does not have sufficient periods of coverage to satisfy the requirements for entitlement to benefits under United States laws, the agency of the United States shall take into account, for the purpose of establishing entitlement to benefits under this Article, periods of coverage which are credited under Icelandic laws and which do not coincide with periods of coverage already credited under United States laws.[42]
2. In determining eligibility for benefits under paragraph 1 of this Article, the agency of the United States shall credit one (1) quarter for every three (3) months of coverage certified by the Iceland; however, no quarter of coverage shall be credited for any calendar quarter already credited as a quarter of coverage under United States laws. The total number of quarters of coverage to be credited for a year shall not exceed four (4). The agency of the United States shall not take into account periods of e which occurred prior to the earliest date for which of coverage may be credited under its laws, nor will the agency of the United States take into account any periods of coverage which are not based on wages or self-employment income.[43]

---

[42] Article 7 contains rules for using combined coverage to determine U.S. benefit eligibility and amounts. If a person has at least six U.S. quarters of coverage, but not enough quarters to qualify for U.S. benefits, SSA will take into account any periods of that Icelandic laws credit, if these periods do not coincide quarters of coverage that the United States already credited. The corresponding Icelandic benefit Article, Article 8.1, provides that rhe Icelandic agencies will consider periods of coverage completed under the U.S. Social Security system for purposes of Icelandic benefit eligibility.

[43] Article 7.2 establishes how SSA will convert periods of under the Icelandic system into equivalent periods under the system. The U.S. system measures periods of coverage in tenns of calendar quarters while the Icelandic system measures periods of coverage in months. Beginning in 1978, SSA bases quarters of coverage on the amount of a person's annual earnings (e.g., for 2013. $1,160 in earnings equals one quarter of coverage). Under Article 7.2, SSA will credit one quarter of coverage in a calendar year for every three months of coverage that the Icelandic agency certifies for that year. SSA will not credit months of coverage under Icelandic laws that fall within a calendar quarter that SSA already credited as a U.S. quarter of coverage. SSA will also not credit more than 4 quarters of coverage for any calendar year or consider of Icelandic coverage credited prior to 1937, the earliest date for which U.S. law permits crediting periods of coverage.

3. Where entitlement to a benefit under United States laws is established according to the provisions of paragraph 1 of this Article, the agency of the United States shall compute a pro rata Primary Insurance Amount in accordance with United States laws based on (a) the person's average earnings credited exclusively under United States laws and (b) the ratio of the duration of the person's periods of coverage completed under United States laws to the duration of a coverage lifetime as determined in accordance with United States laws. Benefits payable under United States laws shall be based on the pro rata Primary Insurance Amount.[44]
4. Entitlement to a benefit from the United States which results from I of this Article shall terminate with the acquisition of periods of coverage under United States laws to establish entitlement to an equal or higher benefit without the need to invoke the provision of paragraph I of this Article.[45]

Article 8: Benefits under Icelandic Laws

The following provisions shall apply to Iceland:
As regards the national old-age and invalidity pension scheme[46]:

---

[44] Article 7.3 describes the method of computing U.S. benefit amounts when SSA establishes entitlement by totalizing (i.e., combining) U.S. and Icelandic coverage. Persons whose U.S. coverage alone qualifies them for U.S. benefits will not receive U.S. totalization benefits. Under Article 7.3, the amount of the worker's benefit depends on both a worker's earnings and the duration of his or her U.S. Social Security coverage. SSA regulations (20 CFR404.1918) describe this computation procedure in detail. The first step in the procedure is to compute a theoretical Primary Insurance Amount (Pl.A) as though the worker had spent a full career under U.S. Social Security at the same level of earnings as during his or her actual periods of U.S. covered work. SSA then prorates the theoretical PIA to reflect the proportion of a coverage lifetime completed under the U.S. program. The regulations define a coverage lifetime as the number of years used in determining a worker's average earnings under the regular U.S. national computation method.

[45] Article 7.4 provides that if a worker entitled to a U.S. totalization benefit earns additional U.S. coverage that enables the worker to qualify for an equal or higher benefit based only on his or her U.S. coverage, SSA will pay the regular national law benefit rather than the totalization benefit.

[46] Iceland pays social security benefits to applicable eligibility standards, including residency and other requirements. Under Article 8, Iceland person's U.S. coverage to his or her periods of Icelandic residency, if necessary, to meet eligibility rules. If the person meets the requirements based on combined U.S. and Icelandic credits, Iceland will pay a benefit in accordance with its laws (see Article 2.1(b)) on national old-age and invalidity benefits.

1. Where a person covered by this Agreement who is or has been to the laws of the United States has had a total period of under Icelandic laws of at least twelve (12) months but does not have

---

ICELANDIC SOCIAL SECURITY BENEFITS GENERAL
The Icelandic social security system is a three-pillar structure. The first pillar consists of a mandatory, residence-based, means tested benefit financed through general government revenues. The second pillar is a fully funded system invested in individual pension funds (mandatory for all wage earners and self-employed persons in Iceland). The voluntary third pillar is an option for employers their employees to make tax-deductible contributions to a pension fund.
This Article applies to the first pillar system, which is a residence-based program that covers all residents of Iceland. Iceland pays benefits under the first pillar in amounts that it bases on the number of years of residency in Iceland. The second and third pillars exist to supplement the basic benefit. For people with low income, including all income from earnings, pensions, and other sources, a number of means tested supplements can increase the amount of the first pillar benefit. These supplements are a form of social assistance, and are only payable to residents of Iceland. Benefits and contributions under the second and third pillar schemes vary according to the funds in which an employee invests, and the government provides general oversight.

OLD-AGE BENEFITS
Retirement age in Iceland is age 67. The Icelandic system requires a minimum of 3 years of residency in Iceland for entitlement to an old-age benefit. A person may retire early at age 65 with a reduced benefit amount, and may elect to defer receipt of his or her benefit until age 70, at which point he or she will be eligible for a higher benefit amount. Iceland pays a flat rate benefit depending on the number of years of residency in Iceland, with 40 years of yielding the maximum benefit amount. A means tested system of benefit supplements for low income beneficiaries, supplements for income level and caring for dependents, increases the basic benefit amount.

DISABILITY BENEFITS
Iceland pays disability benefits to people between ages 18 and 67 who resided in Iceland for 3 years prior to applying for a benefit (or 6 months if they were not disabled when they residence in Iceland) and are assessed to have a permanent recognized disability of at least 75% of working Icelandic system calculates the benefit amount for benefit in a similar manner to the old-age benefit, with same means-tested supplements applying. However, an age-related supplement applies, with residents who became disabled at an earlier age receiving a progressively higher supplement.

SURVIVORS BENEFITS
Most survivors benefits in Iceland take the form of social assistance. However, a flat rate child's benefit is available to a child under the age of 18 whose parent is disabled or deceased, provided that either the child or at least one parent resided in Iceland for at least 3 years.
The child's benefit amount is doubled if both parents are disabled or deceased.
COST-OF-LIVING ADJUSTMENTS
Iceland provides annual cost of living adjustments in its national budget legislation. Benefits increase according to wage indexation, subject to a minimum increase equal to the annual change in the Consumer Price Index.

sufficient periods of coverage to satisfy the requirements for entitlement to benefits under the Icelandic Social Security Act, the agency of Iceland shall take into account for the purpose of entitlement to benefits under this Article, periods of coverage which are credited under United States laws and which do not coincide with periods of coverage already credited under Icelandic law.[47]

2. Where the condition of paragraph I of this Article is fulfilled, a person covered by this Agreement shall be entitled to an Icelandic national pension subject to the other conditions set forth in the Icelandic Social Security Act.[48]

3. Where the condition on work under paragraph 1 of this Article has not been met, a person covered by this Agreement shall be entitled to an Icelandic national pension if the person has been resident in Iceland for a period of not less than three (3) years in the qualifying period laid down in the Icelandic Social Security Act.[49]

4. National old age pension and the invalidity pension shall be payable to persons covered by this Agreement residing in the

---

[47] Article 8 contains rules for determining Icelandic benefit eligibility and amounts for people who have periods of social security coverage in both countries; but who do not have enough Icelandic coverage to for Icelandic benefits. In such cases, the Icelandic agency will add U.S. quarters of coverage to periods of Icelandic coverage in determining whether a person meets the minimum requirements for benefits under Icelandic law.
Under Article 8.1, the Icelandic agency will not take U.S. coverage into account under this Agreement if the worker than 12 months of Icelandic coverage and cannot establish entitlement to Icelandic benefits based on Icelandic coverage alone. Like the similar six quarters of coverage required for totalization by the United States under Article 7.1, this provision removes the considerable administrative burden of processing claims for very small benefits based on minimal periods of coverage. The Icelandic agency will, however, credit U.S. periods of coverage totaling less than six quarters.

[48] Article 8.2 provides that when the Icelandic agency entitles a person to a benefit under Article 8.1 of this Agreement, then the agency will pay that person pursuant to its own national social security laws.

[49] This provision stipulates that if a person cannot be entitled to a benefit using combined coverage from Iceland and the United States, then he or she can be entitled to a benefit under the ordinary rules set forth in the Jaws of Iceland.

territory of the United States if the person concerned fulfills the condition in paragraph 1 of this Article.[50]
5. For purposes of meeting the twelve (12)-month work requirement of paragraph 1 of this Article, the periods of coverage defined in shall be accepted.[51]
6. Periods described in Article 1.1(e)(i-iii) may be combined for purposes of meeting the twelve (12)-month work requirement in paragraph I of this Article.[52]

As regards the Mandatory Pension Insurance Scheme (Pension Funds):

1. Article 19, paragraph 4 of the Act on Mandatory Pension Insurance and on the Activities of Pension Funds shall not apply to contributions paid by a person covered by this Agreement into a Pension Fund operating under such Act on the return of or transfer of residence of that person to the United States.[53]
2. A person covered by this Agreement shall be entitled to a pension in pursuance of the Act on Mandatory Pension Insurance and on the Activities of Pension Funds and the Articles of Association of the relevant Pension Fund, on the basis of contributions paid into a Pension Fund operating under said Act.[54]

---

[50] Under Article 8.4, Iceland will pay beneficiaries residing in the United States when that person's entitlement is established combined U.S. and Icelandic coverage. Separate provisions already commit Iceland to pay national law benefits to residents and citizens of the United States (see Articles 4 and 21.6, respectively).

[51] Article 8.5 specifies that only periods of coverage as defined in Article 1.1(e) will qualify for purposes of meeting the 12 month minimum contribution requirement for entitlement to a Icelandic benefit using combined U.S. and Icelandic coverage.

[52] Expanding on the concept of Article 8.5, this provision clarifies that Iceland can combine different periods of contributions in Article 1.1(e) for the purposes of meeting the mandatory contribution requirement.

[53] Article 19, paragraph 4 of the Act on Mandatory Pension Insurance provides for lump-sum refunds of contributions for foreign nationals upon their permanent departure from Iceland, unless an international agreement provides otherwise. Because it is generally more advantageous for a person to receive totalized monthly benefits instead of a lump-sum refund of contributions, Article that U.S. nationals returning to the United States from take the totalized benefit.

[54] Under Article 8.8, an Icelandic pension fund can pay benefits to any person to whom this Agreement applies regardless of his or her citizenship or country of residence. Under current law, only residents of Iceland are eligible to receive a pension based on

Part IV. Miscellaneous Provisions

Article 9: Administrative Measures

The Competent Authorities of the two Contracting States shall:

a. make all necessary administrative arrangements for the implementation of this Agreement and designate liaison agencies;[55]
b. communicate to each other information concerning the measures taken for the application of this Agreement; and
c. communicate to each other, as soon as possible, information concerning all changes in their respective laws which may affect the application of this Agreement.

Article 10: Mutual Assistance

The Component Authorities and the agencies of the Contracting States, within the scope of their respective authorities, shall assist each other in implementing this Agreement. This assistance shall be free of charge, subject to exceptions to be agreed upon in an administrative arrangement.[56]

Article 11: Confidentiality of Exchanged Personal Data

1. Unless otherwise required by the national statutes of a Contracting State, personal data transmitted in accordance with this Agreement

---

contributions to a Pension Fund. Residents of other countries instead receive a refund of the contributions they previously made to the Pension Fund.

[55] Article 9 outlines various duties of the Competent Authorities under this Agreement. Paragraph (a) authorizes and requires the Competent Authorities to conclude an Administrative and take all necessary administrative measures to implement this Agreement. Paragraph (b) requires them to notify each other of steps they take unilaterally to implement this Agreement. Paragraph (c) obligates the Competent Authorities to other of any changes in their social security Jaws that may application of this Agreement.

[56] Article 10 authorizes the two countries to furnish each non-reimbursable assistance in administering this agreement. Such assistance may include taking benefit applications and the gathering and exchange, including the electronic exchange, of information relevant to claims filed and benefits paid under this Agreement. Although Article 10 establishes a general principle that mutual administrative assistance will be free of charge, the provision authorizes the two sides to agree to exceptions, such as the exception in Article 7.3 of the Administrative Arrangement.

to one Contracting State by the other Contracting State shall be used solely for purposes of administering this Agreement and the laws in Article 2 of this Agreement. The receiving Contracting State's national statutes for the protection of privacy and confidentiality of personal data and the provisions of this Agreement shall govern such use.[57]

2. The Competent Authorities of the Contracting States shall inform each other about all amendments to their national statutes regarding the protection of privacy and confidentiality of personal data that affect the transmission of personal data.[58]

3. A person may request, and the Competent Authority or agency requesting or transmitting personal data pursuant to this Agreement must disclose to that person upon such request, the content, receiving agency, and duration of use of his or her personal data, and the purpose and legal grounds for which such personal data were used or requested.[59]

4. The agencies shall take all reasonable steps to ensure that transmitted personal data are accurate and limited to data required to fulfill the receiving agency's request. In accordance with their respective national statutes, the agencies shall correct or delete any inaccurate transmitted personal data and any data not required to

---

[57] Both the United States and Iceland recognize the great importance of ensuring the integrity of personal data, as well as a person's rights pertaining thereto. Accordingly, both countries have statutes and regulations that govern disclosure and provide strict safeguards for maintaining the confidentiality of personal data in the possession of their respective governments. In the United States, these statutes include the Freedom of Information Act, the Privacy Act, section 6103 of the Internal Revenue Code, and pertinent provisions of the U.S. Act and other related statutes. In Iceland, the applicable laws include Act No. 77/2000 on the Protection of Privacy as regards the Processing of Personal Data (as amended) and EU Directive 95/46/EC (with which Iceland, as a member of the European Economic Area, complies). Article 11.1 provides that both countries will protect personal data furnished under this Agreement in accordance with the applicable provisions of the privacy and confidentiality laws of the country that receives the personal data.

[58] Article 11.2 provides that if either country modifies any of its statutes that regulate the privacy or confidentiality of transmitted between the countries, the Competent Contracting State that modified its statute must Competent Authority of the other Contracting State.

[59] Article 11.3 protects a person's right to request particular information about any of his or her personal data requested from or transmitted to either country under this Agreement. Article I I.3 also provides that when a person requests such information about his or her personal data from a country, that country must provide the requested information to the person.

Agreement on Social Security ... 25

fulfill the receiving agency's request, and immediately notify the other Contracting State's agency of such correction. This shall not limit a person's right to request such correction of his or her personal data directly from the agencies.[60]

5. Both the transmitting and the receiving agencies shall effectively personal data against unauthorized or illegal access, alteration or disclosure.[61]

Article 12: Confidentiality of Exchanged Employers' Information

Unless otherwise required by the national statutes of a Contracting State, information transmitted between Contracting States in accordance with this Agreement shall be used solely for purposes of administering this Agreement and the laws in Article 2 of this Agreement. The receiving Contracting State's national statutes for the protection and of employers' information and the provisions of this Agreement shall govern such use.[62]

Article 13: Documents

1. Where the laws of a Contracting State provide that any document which is submitted to the Competent Authority or an agency of that Contracting State shall be exempted, wholly or partly, from fees or charges, including consular and administrative fees, the exemption shall also apply to corresponding documents which are

---

[60] Article 11.4 provides that both countries will take reasonable steps to ensure the accuracy of personal data transmitted between the two countries and will limit the transmission of personal data to only that information necessary to satisfy the other country's request. However, if one country later discovers that it transmitted or received inaccurate personal data or' personal data not required to satisfy a country's request, the country that discovers the discrepancy will correct or delete the personal data in question and immediately notify the agency of the other country. The countries will perform such correction or deletion in accordance with their respective statutes governing alteration and destruction of data.
Article 11.4 also recognizes the right of a person to ask either agency directly to correct or delete any of his or her own personal data that he or she discovers to be inaccurate or not Contracting State's request.

[61] Both the United States and Iceland agree to protect the integrity, privacy, and confidentiality of personal data under their respective laws when receiving or transmitting such data under this Agreement.

[62] Article 12 provides protections for employers' confidential information. It provides to any business-related information exchanged under this Agreement similar protections to those provided for personal data under this Agreement and under each country's national statutes.

to the Competent Authority or an agency of the other Contracting State in the application of this Agreement.[63]
2. Copies of documents certified as true and exact copies by an agency of one Contracting State shall be accepted as true and exact copies by an agency of the other Contracting State, without further certification. The agency of each Contracting State shall be the final judge of the probative value of the evidence submitted to it from whatever source.[64]

Article 14: Correspondence and Language
1. The Competent Authorities and agencies of the Contracting States may correspond directly with each other and with any person, wherever the person may reside, whenever it is necessary for the administration of this Agreement.[65]
2. An application or document may not be rejected by a Competent Authority or agency of a Contracting State solely because it is in the language of the other Contracting State.[66]

Article 15: Applications
1. A written application for benefits filed with an agency of one Contracting State shall protect the rights of the claimants under the laws of the other Contracting State if the applicant requests that it

---

[63] Article 13.1 states that if the laws of one country exempt documents submitted in connection with a social security claim from fees or charges, that exemption will also apply if a country sends such documents to the other country by or on behalf of a claimant or beneficiary.

[64] If the agency of one country certifies that a copy of a document it furnishes to the agency of the other country is a true and exact copy of an original document, the other country will certification. Nevertheless, each country will remain the final judge of the probative value of any documents submitted to it.

[65] Article 14.1 authorizes direct correspondence between the Competent Authorities and agencies of the two countries and between these bodies and any person with whom they may need to communicate.

[66] The Competent Authorities and agencies of each country may not reject an application or document because it is in the language of the other country. SSA already accepts applications and documents written in any language.

be considered an application under the laws of the other Contracting State.[67]
2. If an applicant has filed a written application for benefits with an of one Contracting State and has not explicitly requested application be restricted to benefits under the laws of that Contracting State, the application shall also protect the rights of the claimants under the laws of the other Contracting State if the provides information at the time of filing indicating that the person on whose record benefits are claimed has completed periods of coverage under the laws of the other Contracting State.[68]
3. The provisions of Part III of this Agreement shall apply only to for which an application is filed on or after the date on which this Agreement enters into force.[69]

Article 16: Appeals and Time Limits
1. A written appeal of a determination made by an agency of one Contracting State may be validly filed with an agency of either Contracting State. The appeal shall be decided according to the procedure and laws of the Contracting State whose decision is being appealed.[70]
2. Any claim, notice, or written appeal which, under the laws of one Contracting State, must have been filed within a prescribed period with an agency of that Contracting State, but which is instead filed

---

[67] Article 15.1 provides for situations in which an application filed fer benefits from one country will also be an application for benefits from the other country.
[68] An applicant who files an application with the agency of one country may not always know about his or her benefit rights in the other country. Article 15.2 provides that even if it states no intention to file for benefits in the other country, an application will also the claimants' rights under the other country's laws if the indicates at the time of filing that the worker had coverage other country.
[69] Article 15.3 requires that a person claiming benefits under this Agreement file an application on or after the date this Agreement enters into force.
[70] Both the United States and Iceland have formal procedures for appealing the determinations of their agencies. Under Article 16.1, a claimant may file a written appeal of a decision the agency of one country with the agency of either country. The appropriate agency of the country whose decision an individual is appealing will consider the appeal under its own laws and procedure.

within the same period with an agency of the other Contracting State, shall be considered to have been filed on time.[71]

Article 17: Transmittal of Claims, Notices, and Appeals

In any case to which the provisions of Article 15 or 16, or both, of this the agency to which the claim, notice, or written appeal has ·been submitted shall indicate the date of receipt on the document and transmit it without delay to the liaison agency of the other Contracting State.[72]

Article 18: Currency
1. Payments under this Agreement may be made in the currency of the Contracting State making the payments.[73]
2. In case provisions designed to restrict the exchange or export of are introduced by either Contracting State, the Governments of both Contracting States shall immediately take measures necessary to ensure the transfer of sums owed by either Contracting State under this Agreement.[74]

Article 19: Resolution of Disagreements

Any disagreement regarding the interpretation or application of this agreement shall be resolved by consultation between the Competent Authorities.[75]

---

[71] Article 16.2 provides that when the laws of one country require the submission of a claim, notice, or written appeal within a set time limit, the agency of that country will consider it filed on time if the claimant files it with the agency of the other country within that prescribed time limit.

[72] The agency with which an applicant files a claim, notice, or written appeal under Articles 15 and/or 16 of this Agreement shall transmit it immediately to the agency of the other country. The sending agency will indicate the date on which it received the document.

[73] The agencies may pay benefits under this Agreement in the currency of either country. SSA pays benefits in U.S. dollars. The SIA may pay Icelandic benefits abroad in Icelandic Kronur.

[74] Should either country restrict the exchange of its currency, both Contracting States will take steps to assure the payment of amounts due under this Agreement.

[75] Article 19 requires the Competent Authorities to attempt to resolve any dispute between them regarding this Agreement through consultation or negotiation.

Article 20: Supplementary Agreements

Agreement may be amended in the future by supplementary agreements, which, from their entry into force, shall be considered an integral part of this Agreement. Such agreements may be given retroactive effect if they so specify.[76]

Article 21: Transitional Provisions

1. This Agreement shall not establish any claim to payment of a benefit for any period before the date of entry into force of this Agreement, or to a lump-sum death benefit if the person died before the entry into force of this Agreement.[77]
2. In determining the right to benefits under this Agreement, consideration shall be given to periods of coverage under the laws of both Contracting States and other events that occurred before the entry into force of this Agreement.[78]
3. In applying paragraph 2 or 3, or both, of Article 6 of this Agreement in the case of persons who were sent to work in the territory of a Contracting State prior to the date of entry into force of this Agreement, the period of employment referred to in those paragraphs shall be considered to begin on the date of the entry into force of this Agreement.[79]

---

[76] Article 20 provides that future supplementary agreements may amend this Agreement. After a supplementary agreement becomes effective, it will become an integral part of this Agreement.

[77] The agencies will pay benefits based on this Agreement no earlier than the effective date of this Agreement. Additionally, the United States will not pay a lump-sum death benefit under this Agreement if the person on whose record a claimant files for benefits died prior to this Agreement's entry into force.

[78] In determining benefit eligibility and amounts under this Agreement, Article 21.2 provides that the agencies will consider periods of coverage earned before this Agreement enters into force. The agencies will also consider events relevant to the determination of benefit rights, such as marriage, death, disability, or attainment of a certain age, which happened prior to this Agreement's effective date, However, the United States will not consider periods of Icelandic coverage credited prior to 1937, the earliest date for which U.S. law permits crediting periods of coverage (See Article 7.2).

[79] Article 21.3 provides that the agencies will measure the 5-year period to which paragraph 2 of Article 6 refers beginning no earlier than the date this Agreement enters into force. Thus, for persons to whom Article 6.2 applies who were working in the other country before this Agreement's effective date, the prior period will not count for purposes of the 5-year limit.

4. Determinations concerning entitlement to benefits made before the entry into force of this Agreement shall not affect rights arising under it.[80]
5. The application of this Agreement shall not result in any reduction in the amount of a benefit to which entitlement was established prior to the entry into force of this Agreement.[81]
6. Nothing in this Agreement shall affect the notes concerning the reciprocity of payment of social security benefits exchanged between the United States and Icelandic Governments on December 1, 1980, and April 16, 1981.[82]

Article 22: Duration and Termination
1. This Agreement shall remain in force until the expiration of one calendar year following the year in which written notice of its termination is given by one of the Contracting States to the other Contracting State.[83]
2. If this Agreement is terminated, rights regarding entitlement to or payment of benefits acquired under it shall be retained. The Contracting States shall make arrangements dealing with rights in the process of being acquired.[84]

---

[80] A decision to award or deny a claim either agency renders prior to the effective date of this Agreement will not prevent a from filing a new application for other benefits that may payable because of this Agreement.

[81] Article 21.5 guarantees that the entry into force of this will not result in a reduction in benefits already payable at this Agreement becomes effective.

[82] The exchange of diplomatic notes between the United States and Iceland on December 1, 1980 and April 16, 1981 guarantees that U.S. nationals who are entitled to Icelandic benefits will receive them regardless of where they reside. Based on these notes and in accordance with section 202(t) of the U.S. Act, SSA pays U.S. Social Security benefits to Icelandic nationals regardless duration of their absence from the United States. Article 21.6 provides that the guarantees contained in these diplomatic notes will remain in effect.

[83] Article 22.1 provides for this Agreement to remain in effect until the expiration of one calendar year after the year in which one of the countries provides written notification to the other that it wishes to terminate this Agreement.

[84] If either country terminates this Agreement, a person will retain benefit rights acquired before termination. Special arrangements would dictate the· extent to which each country would recognize benefit rights in the process of being acquired at the time of termination-for example, periods of coverage that had not yet resulted in fully insured status.

Article 23: Entry into Force

This Agreement shall enter into force on the first day of the third month the month in which each Government shall have received from the other Government written notification that it has complied with all statutory and constitutional requirements for the entry into force of this Agreement.[85]

IN WITNESS WHEREOF, the undersigned, being duly authorized thereto, have signed the present Agreement.[86]

DONE at Reykjavik this 27th day of September, 2016, in duplicate in the English and Icelandic languages, both texts being equally authentic.

ADMINISTRATIVE ARRANGEMENT BETWEEN THE COMPETENT AUTHORITIES OF THE UNITED STATES OF AMERICA AND ICELAND FOR THE IMPLEMENTATION OF THE AGREEMENT ON SOCIAL SECURITY BETWEEN THE UNITED STATES OF AMERICA AND ICELAND

The Competent Authority of the United States of America and the Competent Authority of Iceland

In conformity with Article 9(a) of the Agreement on Social Security the United States of America and Iceland of this date, hereinafter referred to as the "Agreement," have agreed as follows:

---

[85] Once each country completes its internal approval process, the two governments will exchange written notifications to that effect. The Agreement will enter into force on the first day of the third month after the month in which both governments have received the other government's written notification.

[86] The U.S. Ambassador to Iceland, Robert Cushman Barber, and the Icelandic Minister of Social Affairs and Housing, signed this Agreement on September 27, 2016 in Reykjavik.

Chapter 1: General Provisions

Article 1

Where terms that appear in the Agreement are used in this Administrative Arrangement, they shall have the same meaning as they have in the Agreement.[87]

Article 2
1. The liaison agencies referred to in Article 9(a) of the Agreement shall be:[88]
    a. for the United States, the Social Security Administration; and
    b. for Iceland, Tryggingastofnun rikisins (Social Insurance Administration).
2. The liaison agencies designated in paragraph I of this Article shall decide upon the joint procedures and methods necessary for the implementation of the Agreement and this Administrative Arrangement.[89]

Chapter II: Provisions on Coverage

Article 3

1. Where the laws of one Contracting State are applicable in accordance with any of the provisions of Article 6 of the Agreement, the agency of that Contracting State, upon request of

---

[87] Article I provides that terms have the same meaning in the Administrative Arrangement as they do in the Agreement.

[88] Article 2.1 designates the agencies in each country responsible for implementing and administering the coverage and benefit provisions of the Agreement. The United States designates the Social Security Administration as its liaison agency, and Iceland designates the Social Insurance Administration as its counterpart liaison agency.

[89] Article 2.2 authorizes and requires the liaison agencies of both countries to agree upon those procedures, methods, and forms they will use for the implementation of the Agreement and Administrative Arrangement.

the employer or self-employed person, shall issue a certificate stating that the employee or self-employed person is subject to those laws and indicating the duration for which the certificate shall be valid. This certificate shall be evidence that the employee or self-employed person is exempt from the laws on compulsory coverage of the other Contracting State.[90]

2. The certificate referred to in paragraph I of this Article shall be issued:[91]
   a. in the United States, by the Social Security Administration; and
   b. in Iceland, by Tryggingastofnun rikisins (Social Insurance Administration).
3. The agency of a Contracting State that issues a certificate referred to in paragraph 1 of this Article shall furnish a copy of the certificate or agreed upon information from the certificate to the liaison agency of the other Contracting State as needed by the agency of the other Contracting State.[92]

---

[90] Under Article 3.1, the agency of the country whose social coverage laws will continue to apply to a person in accordance with the rules in Part II of the Agreement will issue a certificate to that effect when an employer and employee or a self-employed person requests one. Employers and self-employed persons should request certificates before work begins in the other country, whenever possible. The certificate will serve as evidence of the exemption of the person from the coverage laws of the other country when provided to the agency of the other country.

[91] Article 3.2 designates the agencies in each country responsible for issuing certificates of coverage.

[92] Article 3.3 provides that the agency issuing a coverage certificate will furnish a copy of the certificate or information from the certificate to the liaison agency in the other country when needed.

Chapter III. Provisions on Benefits

Article 4

1. Applications for benefits under the Agreement shall be submitted on forms to be developed by the liaison agencies of the two Contracting States.[93]
2. The agency of the Contracting State, with which an application for benefits is first filed in accordance with Article 15 of the Agreement, shall provide the liaison agency of the other Contracting State with such evidence and other information in its possession as may be required to complete action on the claim.[94]
3. The agency of a Contracting State, which receives an application that was first filed with an agency of the other Contracting State, shall without delay provide the liaison agency of the other Contracting State with such evidence and other available information in its possession as may be required for it to complete action on the claim.
4. The agency of the Contracting State with which an application for benefits has been filed shall verify the information pertaining to the applicant and the applicant's family members. The liaison of both Contracting States shall decide upon the types of information to be verified.[95]

---

[93] The U.S. and Icelandic agencies will agree on forms that people who wish to file for Agreement will use.

[94] Articles 4.2 and 4.3 outline the procedures both countries will follow for the exchange of evidence and information they need to process claims filed under the Agreement.

[95] Article 4.4 deals with the verification of claims information. Both U.S. and Icelandic laws require verification of certain information about individuals claiming benefits (e.g., age and family relationship to the worker) before either country can approve the claim. Article 4.4 provides that when a person files a claim for benefits under the Agreement in one country, the agency of that country will verify the relevant information and inform the agency of the other country of its findings. The liaison agencies will agree upon the specific types of information requiring verification. This provision expedites the claims process by avoiding duplicate verification of the same information. An agency may still request additional evidence to support the finding of the other agency.

Chapter IV. Miscellaneous Provisions

Article 5

1. In accordance with measures to be decided upon pursuant to paragraph 2 of Article 2 of this Administrative Arrangement, the agency of one Contracting State shall, upon request by the agency of the other Contracting State; furnish available information relating to the claim of any specified individual for the purpose of administering the Agreement.[96]
2. For the purpose of facilitation of the implementation of the Agreement and this Administrative Arrangement, the liaison agencies may agree on measures for the provision and transmission of the electronic exchange of data.[97]

Article 6

The liaison agencies of the two Contracting States shall exchange statistics on the number of certificates issued under Article 3 of this Administrative Arrangement and on the payments made to beneficiaries the Agreement. These statistics shall be furnished annually in a manner to be decided upon.[98]

Article 7

1. Where administrative assistance is requested and provided under Article 10 of the Agreement, expenses other than regular personnel and operating costs of the agency providing the assistance shall be

---

[96] Article 5.1 provides that the agency of one country will, request, furnish claims-related information to the agency of the country in accordance with agreed upon procedures. Such procedures will be agreed upon by the agencies and will be consistent with the governing statutes of both countries.

[97] Under Article 5.2, the liaison agencies of both countries may agree to implement electronic data exchanges to facilitate administration of the Agreement and this Administrative Arrangement. Such exchanges must comply with the laws of each country governing the protection of privacy and confidentiality of personal data.

[98] Article 6 provides for an exchange of statistics concerning benefit payments and certificates of coverage made by both countries. This information will include the total number of beneficiaries paid under the Agreement and total payments to these beneficiaries.

reimbursed, except as may be decided by the Competent Authorities or liaison agencies of the Contracting States.[99]
2. Upon request, the liaison agency of either Contracting State shall furnish without cost to the liaison agency of the other Contracting State any medical information and documentation in its possession relevant to the disability of the claimant or beneficiary.[100]
3. Where the agency of a Contracting State requires that a person in the territory of the other Contracting State who is receiving or for benefits under the Agreement submit to a medical examination, such examination, if requested by that agency, shall be arranged by the liaison agency of the other Contracting State in accordance with the ·rules of the agency making the arrangements and at the expense of the agency which requests the examination.[101]
4. The liaison agency of one Contracting State shall reimburse amounts owed under paragraphs 1 or 3 of this Article upon presentation of a statement of expenses by the liaison agency of the other Contracting State.[102]

---

[99] In accordance with Article I 0 of the Agreement, the agencies of the two countries will provide each other with administrative assistance required to implement the Agreement. Under Article 7.1, the requesting agency will pay expenses the other agency incurs in responding to requests for administrative assistance that require it to outside its own organization unless the two countries agree on a arrangement. This includes hiring interpreters, conducting special field investigations, or arranging medical examinations. The agencies will not reimburse expenses for regular personnel and operating costs.

[100] When the liaison agency in one country requests medical information from the liaison agency in the other country, the other liaison agency will provide the requesting liaison agency with any pertinent medical records it has in its possession free of charge.

[101] Article 7.3 provides that where a medical examination is to establish eligibility for or continuing entitlement to a country's benefits that are payable under the Agreement, and the claimant or beneficiary is in the other country, the liaison agency of the other country, upon request, will arrange for the examination at the expense of the agency requesting the examination.

[102] In order to receive reimbursement for the cost of administrative assistance, the liaison agency that provides the assistance must provide the requesting liaison agency with a detailed statement of expenses.

Article 8
1. This Administrative Arrangement shall enter into force on the date of entry into force of the Agreement and shall remain in force so long as the Agreement is in force.[103]
2. The Competent Authorities may notify each other, in writing, of changes in the names of the agencies without the need to amend the Agreement or this Administrative Arrangement.[104]

The United States of America and Iceland (hereinafter referred to as the "Contracting States"), Being desirous of regulating the relationship between their two countries in the field of Social Security, have agreed as follows:

Part I: General Provisions

Article 1: Definitions
For the purposes of this Agreement:
(a) "national" means,
   i. as regards the United States, a national of the United States as defined in Section 101, Immigration and Nationality Act, as amended, and
   ii. as regards Iceland, a national of Iceland as defined in the Icelandic Nationality Act No W0/1952;
(b) "laws" means the laws and regulations specified in Article 2 of this Agreement;
(c) "Competent Authority" means,
   i. as regards the United States, the Commissioner of Social Security, and
   ii. as regards Iceland, velferdarraduneytid (Ministry of Welfare);

---

[103] Article 8.1 provides that this Administrative Arrangement will enter into force on the same date as the Agreement and will remain in effect for the same period as the Agreement.
[104] Under Article 8.2, if the name of an agency in a Contracting State changes, that Contracting State can notify the other Contracting State of such change without the need to amend the Agreement and this Administrative Arrangement.

(d) "agency" means,
   i. as regards the United States, the Social Security Administration, and
   ii. as regards Iceland,
   iii. for the national pension, Tryggingastofuun rikisins (Social Insurance Administration), and
   iv. for the Mandatory Pension Insurance Scheme, the relevant Pension Fund;

(e) "period of coverage" means,
   i. as regards the United States, a period of payment of contributions or a period of earnings from employment or self-employment, as defined or recognized as a period of coverage by the laws under which such period has been completed, or any similar period insofar as it is recognized by such laws as equivalent to a period of coverage; and
   ii. as regards Iceland, residence as defined in section II of the Icelandic Social Security Act, which coincides with
      (i) periods of work or self-employment for which social security or Pension Fund contributions were paid in respect of the laws specified in Article 2(l)(b) of this Agreement,
      (ii) periods before the entry into force of the Act mentioned in subparagraph (e)(i) of this Article for which a person establishes that he or she worked under Icelandic laws, and
      (iii) periods for which a person establishes that he or she was self-employed under Icelandic laws;

(f) "benefit" means any benefit provided for in the laws specified in Article 2 of this Agreement; and

(g) "personal data" means any information relating to a specific (identified or identifiable) person, as well as any information which can be used to distinguish or trace an individual's identity. This includes, but is not limited to, the following: any individual identifier; citizenship, nationality, statelessness or refugee status; benefits, eligibility, or other claims information; contact information; medical information or lay information used in a

medical determination; information about marital, familial or personal relationships; and information pertaining to work, financial or economic status.
1. Any term not defined in this Article shall have the meaning assigned to it in the applicable laws.

Article 2: Material Scope
1. For the purposes of this Agreement, the applicable laws arc:
   (a) as regards the United States, the laws governing the Federal old-age, survivors, and disability insurance program:
       (i) Title II of the U.S. Social Security Act and regulations pertaining thereto, except sections 226, 226A, and 228 of that title, and regulations pertaining to those sections, and
       (ii) Chapters 2 and 21 of the U.S. Internal Revenue Code of 1986 and regulations pertaining to those chapters;
   (b) as regards Iceland, the laws governing the national old-age and invalidity pension scheme and the Mandatory Pension Insurance Scheme (Pension Funds):
       (i) Section II and Section III of the Icelandic Social Security Act and regulations pertaining thereto, except Article 19; Article 20, paragraphs 3 and 4; and Article 18, paragraph 4, second sentence,
       (ii) The Act on Mandatory Pension Insurance and on the Activities of Pension Funds and regulations pertaining thereto, except Article 15, paragraphs 2 and 3, and
       (iii) The Icelandic Social Security Contribution Act.
2. Unless otherwise provided in this Agreement, the laws referred to in paragraph 1 of this Article shall not include treaties or other international agreements or supranational legislation on social security concluded between one Contracting State and a third State, or laws or regulations promulgated for their specific implementation.

3. Except as provided in the following sentence, this Agreement shall also apply to legislation which amends or supplements the laws specified in paragraph 1 of this Article. This Agreement shall apply to future legislation of a Contracting State which creates new categories of beneficiaries or new benefits under the laws of that Contracting State unless the Competent Authority of that Contracting State notifies the Competent Authority of the other Contracting State in writing within three (3) months of the date of the official publication of the new legislation that no such extension of this Agreement is intended.

Article 3: Persons Covered

This Agreement shall apply to:

(a) persons who are or who have been subject to the laws of one or both Contracting States, and
(b) other persons with respect to the rights they derive from the persons·described in sub-paragraph (a) of this Article.

Article 4: Equality of Treatment

Unless otherwise provided in this Agreement, a person designated in Article 3 of this Agreement who resides in the territory of a Contracting State shall receive equal treatment with nationals of the other Contracting State in the application of the laws of the other Contracting State regarding entitlement to or payment of benefits.

Article 5: Portability of Benefits

Unless otherwise provided in this Agreement, any provision of the laws of a Contracting State which restricts entitlement to or payment of benefits solely because a person resides outside or is absent from the territory of that Contracting State shall not be applicable to a person who resides in the territory of the other Contracting State.

Part II: Provisions Concerning Applicable Laws

Article 6: Coverage Provisions
1. Except as otherwise provided in this Article, a person employed within the territory of one of the Contracting States shall, with respect to that employment, be subject to the laws of only that Contracting State.
2. (a) Where a person who is normally employed in the territory of the United States by an employer in that territory is sent by that employer to the territory of Iceland for a temporary period, the person shall be subject to the laws of only the United States as if the person were employed in the territory of the United States, provided that the period of employment in the territory of Iceland is not expected to exceed five (5) years. For purposes of applying this paragraph in the case of an employee who is sent from the territory of the United States by an employer in that territory to the territory of Iceland, that employer and an affiliated company of the employer (as defined under the laws of the United States) shall be considered one and the same, provided that the employment would have been covered under United States laws absent this Agreement.
    (b) Where a person who is resident in the territory of Iceland and employed by an employer whose registered office or place of business is situated in that territory is sent by that employer from that territory to the territory of the United States for a temporary period, the person shall be subject to the laws of only Iceland as if the person were employed and resident in the territory of Iceland, provided that the period of employment in the territory of the United States is not expected to exceed five (5) years.
    (c) If, under subparagraph (a) or (b) of this paragraph, a person continues to be subject to the laws of a Contracting State while in the territory of the other Contracting State, that subparagraph shall also apply to the person's family members

who accompany the person, unless they are themselves employed or self-employed in the territory of the latter Contracting State.

3. Paragraph 2 of this Article shall apply where a person who has been sent by his or her employer from the territory of a Contracting State to the territory of a third State, and who is compulsorily covered under the laws of that Contracting State while employed in the territory of the third State, is subsequently sent by that employer from the territory of the third State to the territory of the other Contracting State.

4. A self-employed person who resides within the territory of a Contracting State shall be subject to the laws of only that Contracting State.

5. Where the same activity is considered to be self-employment under the laws of one Contracting State and employment under the Jaws of the other Contracting State, that activity shall be subject to the laws of only the first Contracting State if the person is a resident of that Contracting State, and to the laws of only the other Contracting State in any other case.

6.
    (a) A person who is employed as an officer or member of a crew on a vessel which flies the flag of one Contracting State and who would be covered under the laws of both Contracting States shall be subject to the laws of only the Contracting State whose flag the vessel flies.

    For purposes of the preceding sentence, a vessel which flies the flag of the United States is one defined as an American vessel under the laws of the United States.

    (b) Traveling employees of air transportation companies who perform work in the territories of both Contracting States and who would otherwise be covered under the laws of both Contracting States shall, with respect to that work, be subject to the laws of only the Contracting State in the territory of which the company has its headquarters. However, if such

Agreement on Social Security ... 43

employees reside in the territory of the other Contracting State, they shall be subject to the laws of only that Contracting State.

7.
   (a) This Agreement shall not affect the provisions of the Vienna Convention on Diplomatic Relations of April 18, 1961, or of the Vienna Convention on Consular Relations of April 24, 1963.
   (b) Nationals of one of the Contracting States who are employed by the Government of that Contracting State in the territory of the other Contracting State but who are not exempt from the laws of the other Contracting State by virtue of the Conventions mentioned in subparagraph (a) of this paragraph shall be subject to the laws of only the first Contracting State. For the purpose of this paragraph, employment by the United States Governnlent includes employment by an instrumentality thereof, and employment by the Icelandic Government includes employment by Icelandic public employers.

8.
   (a) Except as otherwise provided in this Part, a person who does not reside in the territory of Iceland shall not be subject to Icelandic laws.
   (b) When a person is subject to the laws of the United States pursuant to this Article, the person and his or her employer are exempt from paying Icelandic social security contributions and contributions to a Pension Fund under the Act on Mandatory Pension Insurance and on the Activities of the Pension Funds.

9. The Competent Authorities of the two Contracting States rmly agree to grant an exception to the provisions of this Article with respect to particular persons or categories of persons, provided that any affected person shall be subject to the laws of one of the Contracting States.

Part III. Provisions on Benefits

Article 7: Benefits under United States Laws
The following provisions shall apply to the United States:

1. Where a person has completed at least six (6) quarters of coverage under United States laws, but does not have sufficient periods of coverage to satisfy the requirements for entitlement to benefits under United States laws, the agency of the United States shall take into account, for the purpose of establishing entitlement to benefits under this Article, periods of coverage which are credited under Icelandic laws and which do not coincide with periods of coverage already credited under United States laws.
2. In determining eligibility for benefits under paragraph I of this Article, the agency of the United States shall credit one (I) quarter of coverage for every three (3) months of coverage certified by the agency of Iceland; however, no quarter of coverage shall be credited for any calendar quarter already credited as a quarter of coverage under United States laws. The total number of quarters of coverage to be credited for a year shall not exceed four (4). The agency of the United States shall not take into account periods of coverage which occurred prior to the earliest date for which periods of coverage may be credited under its laws, nor will the agency of the United States take into account any periods of coverage which are not based on wages or self-employment income.
3. Where entitlement to a benefit under United States laws is established according to the provisions of paragraph 1 of this Article, the agency of the United States shall compute a pro rata Primary Insurance Amount in accordance with United States laws based on (a) the person's average earnings credited exclusively under United States laws and (b) the ratio of the duration of the person's periods of coverage completed under United States laws to the duration of a coverage lifetime as determined in accordance

with United States laws. Benefits payable under United States laws shall be based on the pro rata Primary Insurance Amount.
4. Entitlement to a benefit from the United States which results from paragraph 1 of this Article shall terminate with the acquisition of sufficient periods of coverage under United States laws to establish entitlement to an equal or higher benefit without the need to invoke the provision of paragraph 1 of this Article.

Article 8: Benefits under Icelandic Laws
The following provisions shall apply to Iceland:
As regards the national old-age and invalidity pension scheme:

1. Where a person covered by this Agreement who is or has been subject to the laws of the United States has had a total period of work under Icelandic laws of at least twelve (12) months but does not have sufficient periods of coverage to satisfy the requirements for entitlement to benefits under the Icelandic Social Security Act, the agency of Iceland shall take into account for the purpose of establishing entitlement to benefits under this Article, periods of coverage which are credited under United States laws and which do not coincide with periods of coverage already credited under Icelandic law.
2. Where the condition of paragraph 1 of this Article is fulfilled, a person covered by this Agreement shall be entitled to an Icelandic national pension subject to the other conditions set forth in the Icelandic Social Security Act.
3. Where the condition on work under paragraph t of this Article has not been met, a person covered by this Agreement shall be entitled to an Icelandic national pension if the person has been resident in Iceland for a period of not less than three (3) years in the qualifying period laid down in the Icelandic Social Security Act.
4. National old age pension and the invalidity pension shall be payable to persons covered by this Agreement residing in the

territory of the United States if the person concerned fulfills the condition in paragraph 1 of this Article.
5. For purposes of meeting the twelve (12) month work requirement of paragraph 1 of this Article, the periods of coverage defined in Article 1.1(e)(i-iii) shall be accepted.
6. Periods described in Article 1.1(e)(i-iii) may be combined for purposes of meeting the twelve (12) month work requirement in paragraph 1 of this Article.

As regards the Mandatory Pension Insurance Scheme (Pension Funds):

1. Article 19, paragraph 4 of the Act on Mandatory Pension Insurance and on the Activities of Pension Funds shall not apply to contributions paid by a person covered by this Agreement into a Pension Fund operating under such Act on the return of or transfer of residence of that person to the United States.
2. A person covered by this Agreement shall be entitled to a pension in pursuance of the Act on Mandatory Pension Insurance and on the Activities of Pension Funds and the Articles of Association of the relevant Pension Fund only on the basis of contributions paid into a Pension Fund operating under said Act.

Part IV: Miscellaneous Provisions

Article 9: Administrative Measures
The Competent Authorities of the two Contracting States shall:

(a) make all necessary administrative arrangements for the implementation of this Agreement and designate liaison agencies;
(b) communicate to each other information concerning the measures taken for the application of this Agreement; and

(c) communicate to each other, as soon as possible, information concerning all changes in their respective laws which may affect the application of this Agreement.

Article 10: Mutual Assistance

The Competent Authorities and the agencies of the Contracting States, within the scope of their respective authorities, shall assist each other in implementing this Agreement. This assistance shall be free of charge, subject to exceptions to be agreed upon in an administrative arrangement.

Article 11: Confidentiality of Exchanged Personal Data

1. Unless otherwise required by the national statutes of a Contracting State, personal data transmitted in accordance with this Agreement to one Contracting State by the other Contracting State shall be used solely for purposes of administering this Agreement and the laws in Article 2 of this Agreement. The receiving Contracting State's national statutes for the protection of privacy and confidentiality of personal data and the provisions of this Agreement shall govern such use.
2. The Competent Authorities of the Contracting States shall inform each other about all amendments to their national statutes regarding the protection of privacy and confidentiality of personal data that affect the transmission of personal data.
3. A person may request, and the Competent Authority or agency requesting or transmitting personal data pursuant to this Agreement must disclose to that person upon such request, the content, receiving agency, and duration of use of his or her personal data, and the purpose and legal grounds for which such personal data were used or requested.
4. The agencies shall take all reasonable steps to ensure that transmitted personal data are accurate and limited to data required to fulfill the receiving agency's request. In accordance with their respective national statutes, the agencies shall correct or delete any inaccurate transmitted personal data and any data not required to

fulfill the receiving agency's request, and immediately notify the other Contracting State's agency of such correction. This shall not limit a person's right to request such correction of his or her personal data directly from the agencies.
5. Both the transmitting and the receiving agencies shall effectively protect personal data against unauthorized or illegal access, alteration, or disclosure.

Article 12: Confidentiality of Exchanged Employers' Information

Unless otherwise required by the national statutes of a Contracting State, employers' information transmitted between Contracting States in accordance with this Agreement shall be used solely for purposes of administering this Agreement and the laws in Article 2 of this Agreement. The receiving Contracting State's national statutes for the protection and confidentiality of employers' information and the provisions of this Agreement shall govern such use.

Article 13: Documents
1. Where the laws of a Contracting State provide that any document which is submitted to the Competent Authority or an agency of that Contracting State shall be exempted, wholly or partly, from fees or charges, including consular and administrative fees, the exemption shall also apply to corresponding documents which arc submitted to the Competent Authority or an agency of the other Contracting State in the application of this Agreement.
2. Copies of documents certified as true and exact copies by an agency of one Contracting State shall be accepted as true and exact copies by an agency of the other Contracting State, without further certification. The agency of each Contracting State shall be the final judge of the probative value of the evidence submitted to it from whatever source.

Article 14: Correspondence and Language
1. The Competent Authorities and agencies of the Contracting States may correspond directly with each other and with any person, wherever the person may reside, whenever it is necessary for the administration of this Agreement.
2. An application or document may not be rejected by a Competent Authority or agency of a Contracting State solely because it is in the language of the other Contracting State.

Article 15: Applications
1. A written application for benefits filed with an agency of one Contracting State shall protect the rights of the claimants under the laws of the other Contracting State if the applicant requests that it be considered an application under the laws of the other Contracting State.
2. If an applicant has filed a written application for benefits with an agency of one Contracting State and has not explicitly requested that the application be restricted to benefits under the laws of that Contracting State, the application shall also protect the rights of the claimants under the laws of the other Contracting State if the applicant provides information at the time of filing indicating that the person on whose record benefits are claimed has completed periods of coverage under the laws of the other Contracting State.
3. The provisions of Part III of this Agreement shall apply only to benefits for which mi application is filed on or after the date on which this Agreement enters into force.

Article 16: Appeals and Time Limits
1. A written appeal of a determination made by an agency of one Contracting State may be validly filed with an agency of either Contracting State. The appeal shall be decided according to the procedure and laws of the Contracting State whose decision is being appealed.

2. Any claim, notice, or written appeal which, under the laws of one Contracting State, must have been filed within a prescribed period with an agency of that Contracting State, but which is instead filed within the same period with an agency of the other Contracting State, shall be considered to have been filed on time.

Article 17: Transmittal of Claims, Notices, and Appeals

In any case to which the provisions of Article 15 or 16, or both, of this Agreement apply, the agency to which the claim, notice, or written appeal has been submitted shall indicate the date of receipt on the document and transmit it without delay to the liaison agency of the other Contracting State.

Article 18: Currency
1. Payments under this Agreement may be made in the currency of the Contracting State making the payments.
2. In case provisions designed to restrict the exchange or export of currencies are introduced by either Contracting State, the Governments of both Contracting States shall immediately take measures necessary to ensure the transfer of sums owed by either Contracting State under this Agreement.

Article 19: Resolution of Disagreements

Any disagreement regarding the interpretation or application of this Agreement shall be resolved by consultation between the Competent Authorities.

Article 20: Supplementary Agreements

This Agreement may be amended in the future by supplementary agreements, which, from their entry into force, shall be considered an integral part of this Agreement. Such Agreements may be given retroactive effect if they so specify.

Article 21: Transitional Provisions
1. This Agreement shall not establish any claim to payment of a benefit for any period before the date of entry into force of this Agreement, or to a lump-sum death benefit if the person died before the entry into force of this Agreement.
2. In determining the right to benefits under this Agreement, consideration shall be given to periods of coverage under the laws of both Contracting States and other events that occurred before the entry into force of this Agreement.
3. In applying paragraph 2 or 3, or both, of Article 6 of this Agreement in the case of persons who were sent to work in the territory of a Contracting State prior to the date of entry into force of this Agreement, the period of employment referred to in those paragraphs shall be considered to begin on the date of entry into force of this Agreement.
4. Determinations concerning entitlement to benefits made before the entry into force of this Agreement shall not affect rights arising under it.
5. The application of this Agreement shall not result in any reduction in the amount of a benefit to which entitlement was established prior to the entry into force of this Agreement.
6. Nothing in this Agreement shall affect the notes concerning the reciprocity of payment of social security benefits exchanged between the United States and Icelandic Governments on December 1, 1980, and April 16, 1981.

Article 22: Duration and Termination
1. This Agreement shall remain in force until the expiration of one calendar year following the year in which written notice of its termination is given by one of the Contracting States to the other Contracting State.
2. If this Agreement is terminated, rights regarding entitlement to or payment of benefits acquired under it shall be retained. The

Contracting States shall make arrangements dealing with rights in the process of being acquired.

Article 23: Entry into Force

This Agreement shall enter into force on the first day of the third month following the month in which each Government shall have received from the other Government written notification that it has complied with all statutory and constitutional requirements for the entry into force of this Agreement.

IN WITNESS WHEREOF, the undersigned, being duly authorized thereto, have signed the present Agreement.

DONE at Reykjavik this 27 day of, 2016, in duplicate, in the English and Icelandic languages, both texts being equally authentic.

For The United States of America:

[signature: Robert Cushman Barber]

For Iceland:

[signature]

ADMINISTRATIVE ARRANGEMENT BETWEEN THE COMPETENT AUTHORITIES OF THE UNITED STATES OF AMERICA AND ICELAND FOR THE IMPLEMENTATION OF THE AGREEMENT ON SOCIAL SECURITY BETWEEN THE UNITED STATES OF AMERICA AND ICELAND

The Competent Authority of the United States of America and the Competent Authority of Iceland

In conformity with Article 9(a) of the Agreement on Social Security between the United States of America and Iceland of this date, hereinafter referred to as the "Agreement," have agreed as follows:

Chapter I: General Provisions

Article 1

Where terms that appear in the Agreement are used in this Administrative Arrangement, they shall have the same meaning as they have in the Agreement.

Article 2
1. The liaison agencies referred to in Article 9(a) of the Agreement shall be:
   (a) for the United States, the Social Security Administration; and
   (b) for Iceland, Tryggingastofuun rikisins
       (Social Insurance Administration).
2. The liaison agencies designated in paragraph 1 of this Article shall decide upon the joint procedures and methods necessary for the implementation of the Agreement and this Administrative Arrangement.

Chapter II. Provisions on Coverage

Article 3
1. Where the laws of one Contracting State are applicable in accordance with any of the provisions of Article 6 of the Agreement, the agency of that Contracting State, upon request of the employer or self-employed person, shall issue a certificate stating that the employee or self-employed person is subject to those laws and indicating the duration for which the certificate shall be valid. This certificate shall be evidence that the employee or self-employed person is exempt from the laws on compulsory coverage of the other Contracting State.
2. The certificate referred to in paragraph 1 of this Article shall be issued:

(a) in the United States, by the Social Security Administration; and

(b) in Iceland, by Tryggingastofnun rikisins (Social Insurance Administration).

3. The agency of a Contracting State that issues a certificate referred to in paragraph 1 of this Article shall furnish a copy of the certificate or agreed upon information from the certificate to the liaison agency of the other Contracting State as needed by the agency of the other Contracting State.

Chapter III: Provisions on Benefits

Article 4

1. Applications for benefits under the Agreement shall be submitted on forms to be developed by the liaison agencies of the two Contracting States.

2. The agency of the Contracting State, with which an application for benefits is first filed in accordance with Article 15 of the Agreement, shall provide the liaison agency of the other Contracting State with such evidence and other information in its possession as may be required to complete action on the claim.

3. The agency of a Contracting State, which receives an application that was first filed with an agency of the other Contracting State, shall without delay provide the liaison agency of the other Contracting State with such evidence and other available information in its possession as may be required for it to complete action on the claim.

4. The agency of the Contracting State with which an application for benefits has been filed shall verify the information pertaining to the applicant and the applicant's family members. The liaison agencies of both Contracting States shall decide upon the types of information to be verified.

Chapter IV: Miscellaneous Provisions

Article 5
1. In accordance with measures to be decided upon pursuant to paragraph 2 of Article 2 of this Administrative Arrangement, the agency of one Contracting State shall, upon request by the agency of the other Contracting State, furnish available information relating to the claim of any specified individual for the purpose of administering the Agreement.
2. For the purpose of facilitation of the implementation of the Agreement and this Administrative Arrangements the liaison agencies may agree on measures for the provision and transmission of the electronic exchange of data.

Article 6
The liaison agencies of the two Contracting States shall exchange statistics on the number of certificates issued under Article 3 of this Administrative Arrangement and on the payments made to beneficiaries under the Agreement. These statistics shall be furnished annually in a manner to be decided upon.

Article 7
1. Where administrative assistance is requested and provided under Article 10 of the Agreement, expenses other than regular personnel and operating costs of the agency providing the assistance shall be reimbursed, except as may be decided by the Competent Authorities or liaison agencies of the Contracting States.
2. Upon request, the liaison agency of either Contracting State shall furnish without cost to the liaison agency of the other Contracting State any medical information and documentation in its possession relevant to the disability of the claimant or beneficiary.
3. Where the agency of a Contracting State requires that a person in the territory of the other Contracting State who is receiving or applying for benefits under the Agreement submit to a medical

examination, such examination, if requested by that agency, shall be arranged by the liaison agency of the other Contracting State in accordance with the rules of the agency making the arrangements and at the expense of the agency which requests the examination.

4. The liaison agency of one Contracting State shall reimburse amounts owed under paragraphs 1 or 3 of this Article upon presentation of a statement of expenses by the liaison agency of the other Contracting State.

Article 8

1. This Administrative Arrangement shall enter into force on the date of entry into force of the Agreement and shall remain in force so long as the Agreement is in force.
2. The Competent Authorities may notify each other, in writing, of changes in the names of the agencies without the need to amend the Agreement or this Administrative Arrangement.

DONE at Reykjavik, this 27 day of September, 2016, in duplicate, in duplicate, in the English and Icelandic languages, both texts being equally authentic.

For the Competent Authority of the United States of America:

For the Competent Authority of Iceland:

SOCIAL SECURITY MEMORANDUM

Date: July 8, 2016
Refer To: TCC
To: Stephen C. Goss, ASA, MAAA
Chief Actuary
From: Chris Chaplain, ASA /s/
Supervisory Actuary

Nettie Barrick /s/
Actuary

Subject: Estimated Effects of a Potential Totalization Agreement between Iceland and the United States-

Information

This memorandum and the attached tables present estimates of the effects of implementing a potential totalization agreement with Iceland assuming an effective date of August 1, 2018.

Table 1 shows the estimated net additional program costs to the Social Security systems of the United States (OASDI) and Iceland under the potential agreement for fiscal years 2018 through 2024, the end of the short-range projection period under the 2015 Trustees Report. In each case, these net additional program costs arise under the respective systems due to: (1) benefits payable because of the agreement; and (2) tax contributions for temporary foreign workers eliminated under the agreement.

The first three rows of Table 2 show estimates of the numbers of persons (as of mid-year) who would receive "totalized" benefits from each system. The fourth row of the table shows the number of Icelandic citizens living outside the U.S., and Icelandic residents who are citizens of a third country, who would be affected by removing the 5-year U.S. residency requirement for survivor or dependent benefits. The last two rows of the table show estimates of the numbers of temporary foreign workers in the respective countries who would be exempt from taxation by the local Social Security system under a totalization agreement. Under the agreement, U.S. workers working for a U.S. firm in Iceland for a period expected to last 5 years or less would pay Social Security taxes only to the United States. Icelandic workers working for an Icelandic firm in the U.S. for a period expected to last 5 years or less would pay Social Security taxes only to the Icelandic system. We base estimates shown in the tables on the intermediate set of assumptions of the 2015 OASDI Trustees Report. The exchange rate used in these estimates is 124.900 Iceland krona (JSK) per U.S. dollar (I ISK $0.008006), the exchange rate as of June I, 2016. To provide a frame of reference, the average daily exchange rate over the past 5 years is about 123.320 ISK per U.S. dollar, with a low of about 111.610 ISK per U.S. dollar and a high of about 139.800 ISK per U.S. dollar.

These estimates are subject to much uncertainty. Many of the estimates are based on limited data for Iceland and the assumption that certain relationships that apply on average for other countries where totalization agreements already exist will apply for Iceland as well.

Numbers of Totalized Beneficiaries

To estimate the numbers of totalized beneficiaries under the U.S. Social Security system resulting from an agreement with Iceland, we use two data sources for 21 of the existing agreement countries in a regression analysis.[105] From Census Bureau files, we estimate immigration and

---

[105] We excluded 4 totalization agreement countries from the analysis--the Slovak Republic because the agreement has not been in effect long enough for us to have five full years of data available, South Korea because work before 1986 in South Korea would not be counted as coverage in determining eligibility for totalized benefits, Luxembourg because of lack of data, and Canada because it is a border country with emigrant and immigrant patterns that would likely vary widely from those of Iceland.

emigration. From counts of nonimmigrant visas issued by U.S. Foreign Service posts in each country to persons traveling to the U.S., over a 5-year period roughly 30 years ago when 2018-2024 retirees potentially receiving benefits under the totalization agreement were in their prime working years, we estimate the influx of temporary workers. This analysis yields an estimate of about 170 totalized beneficiaries under the U.S. Social Security system at the end of the 5th year of the potential agreement with Iceland. For 9 of these existing-agreement countries, the predicted number of beneficiaries from the regression is higher than the actual number· at the end of 5 years, by a median value of about 82 percent of the actual number. For 12 of these existing-agreement countries, the predicted number of beneficiaries from the regression is lower than the actual number, by a median value of about 29 percent of the actual number. Therefore, the number of OASDI beneficiaries at the end of the 5th year of implementation would be: (1) about 100, if the median relationship for countries with fewer beneficiaries than predicted by the regression analysis applies to Iceland; and (2) about 240, if the median relationship for countries with more beneficiaries than predicted by the regression applies to Iceland.

To estimate the number of totalized Icelandic beneficiaries under the agreement, we use Census Bureau immigration data to make an initial estimate of the number of beneficiaries who will receive totalized benefits under the Icelandic system. We then adjust this estimate based on a comparison of the number of beneficiaries under the U.S. system estimated using the same data, and the regression estimate for the U.S. system described in the previous paragraph.

Totalization agreements provide OASDI benefits mainly to three groups. The first group is Icelandic non-immigrants (temporary visa holders) who work in the U.S. for less than I 0 years. These workers would have coverage under the U.S. Social Security system (unless they work for an Icelandic firm in the U.S. for 5 years or less after a totalization agreement becomes effective), and may be eligible for U.S. totalized benefits when their work in Iceland is also considered. The second group is legal immigrants (generally permanent) from Iceland to the U.S. who work in the U.S. for less than 10 years, frequently because they immigrate later in their working careers. The third group is emigrants from the U.S. to Iceland (Iceland-born or U.S.-born) who worked in the U.S. for less than 10 years, frequently because they emigrated relatively early in their careers.

A totalization agreement between Iceland and the United States precludes OASDI disability benefits for Icelandic workers employed by an Icelandic employer in the U.S. for 5 years or less who become disabled while working in the U.S. or shortly thereafter. However, temporary workers from Iceland are unlikely to work long enough to qualify for U.S. disability benefits (generally at least 5 years), and are expected to be relatively healthy at the time they come to the U.S. to work. Therefore, we believe that reductions in OASDI disability benefits due to eliminating double taxation under a totalization agreement between Iceland and the United States would be minimal. Similarly, we believe the reductions in disability benefits under the Icelandic system would be very small, relative to removing taxation to the Icelandic system for temporary U.S. workers in Iceland.

5-Year Residency Requirement

In addition to estimates of the number of persons who would receive totalized OASDI benefits, we also estimate the number of alien dependents and survivors who do not meet the 5-year U.S. residency requirement for receipt of Social Security benefits. These individuals would receive OASDI benefits under a totalization agreement because the residency requirement does not apply to totalization countries.

Effects Related to Other US. Social Insurance Programs

The principal financial effects of a totalization agreement apply to the Social Security programs of the countries involved. Totalization agreements do not cover Medicare benefits. Thus, the U.S. cannot use credits for work in Iceland to establish entitlement under the Medicare program. However, the tax side of the U.S. Medicare program would be affected because of the removal of double taxation for Icelandic workers who temporarily work in the U.S. for an Icelandic firm. We do not expect corresponding reduced Medicare outlays, because attainment of Medicare entitlement by these workers is highly unlikely under the current (no totalization) rules. Medicare eligibility is largely restricted to individuals who either: (1) are at least age 65 and eligible for U.S. Social Security benefits; or (2) were entitled to U.S. Social Security disability benefits (as a disabled worker, disabled widow(er), or disabled adult child) for at least 24 months. Furthermore, Medicare reimbursement is generally restricted to services provided in the U.S. Under the current (no totalization) rules, it is unlikely that temporary workers from Iceland would (a) work enough to qualify for Medicare and (b) live in the U.S. when they might avail themselves of Medicare services; therefore, we believe a totalization agreement between Iceland and the United States would reduce Medicare benefits very minimally.

By law, totalization agreements do not affect payroll taxes paid for work injury (workers' compensation) and unemployment programs administered by the United States. Therefore, Icelandic temporary workers employed by Icelandic firms in the U.S., and their employers would still be required to pay any applicable workers' compensation and unemployment payroll taxes. These programs generally operate at the state, and not the federal, level.

Effects Related to Other Icelandic Social Insurance Programs

The Icelandic health insurance program is a non-contributory, tax financed, program. Both with and without a totalization agreement, an individual from the U.S. working temporarily, in Iceland, for a U.S. employer would be eligible for health insurance benefits from the Icelandic system. The employer's contributions to the Icelandic social security system also finance maternity and paternity benefits, sickness benefits, work injury benefits, and unemployment benefits. Under a totalization agreement, U.S. employers of U.S. individuals working temporarily in Iceland would no longer make contributions to these programs, and the Icelandic government would no longer pay benefits to these workers. We believe that most U.S. employers would provide benefits to their employees, such that Icelandic sickness/maternity benefits are rarely paid to these workers. Most U.S. employers would also continue to pay earnings to people incapacitated due to injury for relatively short periods of time, such that Icelandic work injury benefits are rarely paid to these workers. Therefore, we estimate that the value of Icelandic work injury benefits no longer payable to U.S. temporary workers affected by a potential totalization agreement would be very small.

In addition, the Icelandic system would lose unemployment payroll tax contributions from employers affected under a totalization agreement. The Icelandic unemployment program pays benefits for a period of up to 3 years. However, we believe that very few temporary U.S. workers (working for U.S. employers) in Iceland are removed from their jobs, and the few that are removed most likely move back to the United States and do not look for other work in Iceland. Under a potential totalization agreement, U.S. temporary workers in Iceland would no longer be eligible for Icelandic unemployment benefits. Due to the fact that payment of unemployment benefits to temporary U.S. workers in Iceland is unlikely, the value of current unemployment benefits that would no longer be paid by Iceland's system, under a totalization agreement, is expected to be very small.

Long-Range Financial Effects

Table 1. Estimated net additional program costs for the U.S. and Icelandic Social Security (and other) systems under a potential totalization agreement between the two countries, fiscal years 2018-2024 (in millions)

	Fiscal Year							
	2018	2019	2020	2021	2022	2023	2024	Total, FY 2018-24
Financial Effects for the U.S. Social Security system:								
Increase in OASDI benefit payments	1/	1/	1/	1/	1/	$1	$1	$2
Reduction in OASDI tax contributions	1/	$1	$1	$1	$1	1/	1/	4
Net OASDI cost	1/	1	1	1	1	1	1	6
Net cost to the Medicare system	1/	1/	1/	1/	1/	1/	1/	1
Net costs to the Social Security System of Iceland:								
increase in benefit payments	1/	1/	1/	1	1	2	2	6
Reduction in OASDI tax contributions	1/	1	1	1	1	1	1	5
Total	1/	1	1	2	2	2	3	11
1/ Less than $500,000.								

Notes:
1. The agreement is assumed to become effective on August 12018.
2. The estimates are based on the intermediate assumptions of the 2015 Trustees Report.
3. Totals may not equal the sums of the components due to rounding.
4. Estimates arc in U.S. dollars. The assumed exchange rate is 124.900 Iceland krona per U.S. dollar.

Social Security Administration
Office of the Chief Actuary
July 8, 2016

Table 2. Estimated number of persons affected by a potential totalization agreement between the United States and Iceland, fiscal years 2018-2024 (in thousands)

	Fiscal Year						
	2018	2019	2020	2021	2022	2023	2024
Number of persons receiving a totalized OASDI benefit based in part on employment in Iceland (in current-pay status at mid-year)	1/	1/	1	1	1	2	2
Number of persons receiving a totalized Icelandic benefit based in part on employment in the United States (in current-pay status at mid-year)	1/	1/	1	1	1	2	2
Number of persons receiving both a totalized OASDI benefit and a totalized benefit from Iceland (in current-pay status at mid-year)	1/	1/	1/	1/	1/	1/	1/
Number of residents Iceland, or Icelandic citizens living outside the U.S.• who would now be able to receive OASDI dependent or survivor benefits because the 5-year residency requirement would no longer apply (in current-pay status at mid year)	1/	1/	1/	1/	1/	1/	1/
Number of U.S. employees in Iceland who, along with their employers, would no longer make tax contributions during the year to the Social Security system of Iceland	1/	1/	1/	1/	1/	1/	1/
Number of Icelandic employees in the U.S who, along with their employers, would no longer make tax contributions during the year to the OASDHI	1	1	1	1	1	1	1

1/ fewer than 50.
Notes:
1. The agreement is assumed to become effective on August 1, 2018.
2. The estimates are based on the intermediate assumptions of the 2015 Trustees Report.

Social Security Administration
Office of the Chief Actuary
July 8, 2016

Table 3. Projected Not OASDI Cost of Implementing Proposed Totalization Agreement between US and Iceland

Year	Additional OASDI Net Benefits For Year 1/	Change in OASDI Payroll Taxes For Year	Additional OASDI Net Cost For Year 2/	Additional OASDI Net Cost Year 2/	Cumulative Additional OASDI Net Cost 2/
	(Millions of CPI-Indexed 2015$)			(Millions of $, Present Value as of 1-1-15)	
2015	0	0	0	0	0
2016	0	0	0	0	0
2017	0	0	0	0	0
2018	0	0	0	0	0
2019	0	-1	1	1	1
2020	0	-1	1	1	2
2021	0	-1	1	1	2
2022	0	-1	1	1	3
2023	0	-1	1	1	4
2024	0	-1	1	1	5
2025	0	-1	1	1	6
2026	1	-1	1	1	7
2027	1	-1	1	1	8
2028	1	-1	1	1	9
2029	1	-1	1	1	10
2030	1	-1	1	1	11
2031	1	-1	1	1	12
2032	1	-1	1	1	13
2033	1	-1	1	1	14
2034	1	-1	1	1	15
2035	1	-1	1	1	15
2036	1	-1	1	1	16
2037	1	-1	1	1	17
2038	1	-1	1	1	18
2039	1	-1	1	1	19
2040	1	-1	1	1	20
2041	1	-1	1	1	21
2042	1	-1	1	1	21
2043	1	-1	2	1	22
2044	1	-1	2	1	23
2045	1	-1	2	1	24

Year	Additional OASDI Net Benefits For Year 1/	Change in OASDI Payroll Taxes For Year	Additional OASDI Net Cost For Year 2/	Additional OASDI Net Cost Year 2/	Cumulative Additional OASDI Net Cost 2/
	(Millions of CPI-Indexed 2015$)			(Millions of $, Present Value as of 1-1-15)	
2046	1	-1	2	1	25
2047	1	-1	2	1	25
2048	1	-1	2	1	26
2049	1	-1	2	1	27
2050	1	-1	2	1	28
2051	1	-1	2	1	28
2052	1	-1	2	1	29
2053	1	-1	2	1	30
2054	1	-1	2	1	31
2055	1	-1	2	1	31
2056	1	-1	2	1	32
2057	1	-1	2	1	33
2058	1	-1	2	1	33
2059	1	-1	2	1	34
2060	1	-1	2	1	35
2061	1	-1	2	1	35
2062	1	-1	2	1	36
2063	1	-1	2	1	37
2064	1	-1	2	1	37
2065	1	-1	2	1	38
2066	1	-1	2	1	39
2067	1	-1	2	1	39
2068	1	-1	2	1	40
2069	1	-1	2	1	41
2070	1	-1	2	1	41
2071	1	-1	2	1	42
2072	1	-1	2	1	42
2073	1	-1	2	1	43
2074	1	-1	3	1	43
2075	1	-1	3	1	44
2076	1	-1	3	1	45
2077	1	-1	3	1	45
2078	1	-1	3	1	46
2079	1	-1	3	1	46
2080	1	-1	3	1	47
2081	1	-1	3	1	47
2082	1	-1	3	1	48
2083	1	-1	3	1	48
2084	1	-1	3	1	49
2085	1	-2	3	0	49

Table 3. (Continued)

Year	Additional OASDI Net Benefits For Year 1/	Change in OASDI Payroll Taxes For Year	Additional OASDI Net Cost For Year 2/	Additional OASDI Net Cost Year 2/	Cumulative Additional OASDI Net Cost 2/
	(Millions of CPI-Indexed 2015$)			(Millions of $, Present Value as of 1-1-15)	
2086	2	-2	3	0	50
2087	2	-2		0	50
2088	2	-2	3	0	51
2089	2	-2	3	0	51
Based on Intermediate Assumptions of the 2015 Trustees Report. 1/ Additional benefits less revenue to OASDI from taxes on benefits. 2/ Additional net benefit payments minus change in payroll tax revenue.			Social Security Administration Office of the Chief Actuary July 8, 2016		

Implementing the potential totalization agreement between the U.S. and Iceland would decrease the long-range (75-year) actuarial balance of the OASDI program by an amount that is estimated to be negligible (that is, by less than 0.005 percent of taxable payroll).

Table 3 displays the components of the estimated net cost to the OASDI Trust Funds for years 2015 through 2089 on a "CPT-indexed to 2015" basis, i.e., indexing the amounts hack to the year 2015 by assumed changes in the consumer price index (CPI). In addition, the table displays total estimated OASDI net costs on an annual and cumulative present-value basis, i.e., indexing the amounts back to January I, 2015 by projected interest rates earned by the OASDI Trust Funds on special-issue U.S. Government bonds.

In: Agreements on Social Security …
Editor: Jan Kořínek

ISBN: 978-1-53615-219-7
© 2019 Nova Science Publishers, Inc.

Chapter 2

AGREEMENT ON SOCIAL SECURITY BETWEEN THE UNITED STATES AND URUGUAY[*]

Message from the President of the United States

To the Congress of the United States:

Pursuant to section 233(e)(1) of the Social Security Act, as amended by the Social Security Amendments of 1977 (Public Law 95–216, 42 U.S.C. 433(e)(1)), I transmit herewith a social security totalization agreement with Uruguay, titled "Agreement on Social Security between the United States of America and the Oriental Republic of Uruguay," and the accompanying legally binding administrative arrangement, titled "Administrative Arrangement between the Competent Authorities of the United States of America and the Oriental Republic of Uruguay for the Implementation of the Agreement on Social Security between the United States of America and the Oriental Republic of Uruguay" (collectively the

---

[*] This is an edited, reformatted and augmented version of 115th Congress, 2d Session, Publication No. House Document 115–102, dated March 20, 2018.

"Agreements"). The Agreements were signed at Montevideo, Uruguay, on January 10, 2017.

The Agreements are similar in objective and content to the social security totalization agreements already in force with most European Union countries, Australia, Canada, Chile, Japan, Norway, the Republic of Korea, and Switzerland. Such bilateral agreements provide for limited coordination between the United States and foreign social security systems to eliminate dual social security coverage and taxation, and to help prevent the lost benefit protection that can occur when workers divide their careers between two countries.

The Agreements contain all provisions mandated by section 233 of the Social Security Act and, pursuant to section 233(c)(4), other provisions which I deem appropriate to carry out the purposes of section 233.

I also transmit for the information of the Congress a report required by section 233(e)(1) of the Social Security Act on the estimated number of individuals who will be affected by the Agreements and the Agreements' estimated cost effect. Also included are a summary of the main provisions and an annotated version of the Agreements with descriptions of each article. The Department of State and the Social Security Administration have recommended the Agreements to me.

I commend to the Congress the Agreement on Social Security between the United States of America and the Oriental Republic of Uruguay and the Administrative Arrangement between the United States of America and the Oriental Republic of Uruguay for the Implementation of the Agreement on Social Security between the United States of America and the Oriental Republic of Uruguay.

Donald J. Trump
The White House,
March 19, 2018.

AGREEMENT ON SOCIAL SECURITY BETWEEN THE UNITED STATES OF AMERICA AND THE REPUBLIC OF URUGUAY

The United States of America ("United States") and The Oriental Republic of Uruguay ("Uruguay") (hereinafter individually known as Contracting State" or collectively as "Contracting States"),

Being, desirous of regulating the relationship between the two countries in the field of social security, have agreed as follows:

Part I: General Provisions

Article 1: Definitions
1. For the purposes of this Agreement on Social Security between the United States of America and the Oriental Republic of Uruguay (hereinafter "Agreement");
   a) "National" means, as regards the United States, a national of the United States as defined in Section 101, Immigration and Nationality Act, as amended, and as regards Uruguay, natural or·legal citizen as provided for in Articles.73 through 75 of the Constitution of the Republic;
   b) Laws·means the laws and regulations specified in Article 2 of this Agreement;
   c) "Competent Authority" means, as regards the United States, the Commissioner of Social· Security Administration and as regards Uruguay, the Ministerio de Trabajo y Seguridad Social (Ministry of Labor and Social Security), and by delegation, the Banco de Previsión Social (Social Security Bank);
   d) "Competent Institution" means, as regards the United States, the Social Security Administration, and as regards Uruguay, the Banco de Previsión Social (Social Security Bank) the Caja Notarial de Seguridad. Social (Notarial Social Security Fund),

the Caja de Jubilaciones y Pensiones de Profesionales Universitarios (Pension and Retirement Fund of UniversityProfessionals), the Caja de Jubilaciones y Pensiones Bancarias (Banking Pension and Retirement Fund), the Servicio de Retiros y Pensiones Policiales (Police Retirement and Pension Fund), and the Servicio de Retiros y Pensiones de las Fuerzas Armadas (Armed Forces Pension and Retirement Fund);

e) "Liaison Institution" means the organization responsible for coordinating and exchanging information between the Competent Institutions of both Contracting States;

f) "Period of Coverage" means a period of payment of contributions or a period of earnings from employment or self employment, as defined or recognized as a period of coverage by the Laws, under which such period has been completed, or any similar period insofar as it is recognized by such Laws as equivalent to a period of coverage;

g) "Benefit" means any benefit provided for in the Laws specified in Article 2 of this Agreement; and

h) "Personal Data" means any information relating to a specific (identified or identifiable) person, as well as any information that can be used to distinguish or trace an individual's identity. This includes, but is not limited to, the following: any individual identifier; citizenship, nationality, statelessness, or refugee status; benefits, eligibility, or other claims information; contact information; medical information or lay information used in a medical determination; information about marital, familial, or personal relationships; and information pertaining to work, financial, or economic status

2. Any term not defined in this Article shall have the meaning assigned to it in the applicable Laws.

Article 2: Material Scope

1. For the purpose of this Agreement, the, applicable Laws are:
   a) as regards the United States, the laws governing the Federal old-age, survivors, and disability insurance program:
      i. Title II of the Social Security Act and regulations pertaining ·thereto, except sections 226, 226A, and 228 of that title, and regulations pertaining to those sections, and
      ii. Chapters 2 and 21 of the Internal Revenue Code of 1986 and regulations pertaining to those chapters; and
   b) as regards Uruguay, the constitutional, legal and regulatory provisions regarding the contributory benefits for disability, old age and survivors managed by the Banco de Previsión Social (Social Security Bank) the Caja Notarial de Seguridad. Social (Notarial Social Security Fund), the Caja de Jubilaciones y Pensiones de Profesionales Universitarios (Pension and Retirement Fund of UniversityProfessionals), the Caja de Jubilaciones y Pensiones Bancarias (Banking Pension and Retirement Fund), the Servicio de Retiros y Pensiones Policiales (Police Retirement and Pension Fund), and the Servicio de Retiros y Pensiones de las Fuerzas Armadas (Armed Forces Pension and Retirement Fund);
2. Unless otherwise provided in this Agreement, the Laws referred to in paragraph 1 of this Article shall not include treaties or other international agreements or supranational legislation on Social Security concluded between one Contracting State and a third State, or Laws promulgated for their specific implementation.
3. This Agreement shall apply to any amendments to the Laws, including changes to the Laws that extend the provisions of this Agreement in a Contracting State to new categories of beneficiaries or new benefits, unless the Competent Authority of such Contracting State notifies the Competent Authority of the other Contracting State in writing within three (3) months after the

official publication of the new legislation or regulations that no such extension is intended under the terms of this Agreement.

Article 3: Personal Scope

This Agreement shall apply to:

a) persons who are or have been subject to the Laws of one or both Contracting States; and
b) other persons with respect to the rights they derive from the persons described in sub-paragraph (a) of this Article;

Article 4: Equality of Treatment and Portability of Benefits

1. Unless otherwise provided in this Agreement, persons described in Article 3 of this Agreement who reside in the territory of one Contracting State shall receive equal treatment with Nationals of such Contracting State as regards the application of its Laws.
2. Unless otherwise provided in this Agreement, any provision of the Laws of a Contracting State which restricts entitlement to or payment of Benefits solely because a person resides outside or is absent from the territory of that Contracting State shall not be applicable to a person who resides in the territory of the other Contracting State.

Part III: Provisions Concerning Applicable Laws

Article 5: General Rules

Except as otherwise provided in this Part, a person employed or self-employed within the territory of one of the Contracting States, with respect to that employment or self-employment, shall be subject to the Laws of only that Contracting State,

Article 6: Specific Rules

1. Where a person who is normally employed in the territory of one Contracting State by an employer in that territory is sent by that employer to the territory of the other Contracting State for a temporary period that is not expected to exceed five (5) years, the person shall be subject to 'the Laws of only the first Contracting State as if the person were still employed in the territory of the first Contracting State.
2. When a self-employed worker transfers from the territory of one Contracting State to the territory of the other Contracting State for the purpose of performing his or her usual work for a period that is not expected to exceed five (5) years, he or she will be exclusively subject to the Laws of the first Contracting State as if he or she continued working in the territory of the first Contracting State.
3. For purposes of applying paragraph 1 of this Article in the case of an employee who is sent from the territory of a Contracting State by an employer in that territory to the other Contracting State to work for an affiliated company of that employer, that employer and the affiliated company of the employer (as defined under the laws of the Contracting State under which the employer is organized) shall be considered one and the same, provided that, if this Agreement did not exist, the employment would have been covered under the Laws of the Contracting State from which the employee was sent.
4. Paragraphs 1 and 3 of this Article shall apply where a person who has been sent by his or her employer from the territory of a Contracting State to the territory of a third State, and who is compulsorily covered under the Laws of that Contracting State while employed in the territory of the third State, is subsequently sent by that employer from the territory of the third State to the territory of the other Contracting State.

5.
- (a) A person who is employed as an officer or member of a crew on a vessel which flies the flag of one Contracting State and who would be covered under the Laws of both Contracting States shall be subject to, the Laws of only the Contracting State whose flag the vessel flies. For purposes of the preceding sentence a vessel which flies the flag of the United States is one defined as an American vessel under the Laws of the United States.
- (b) Traveling employees of air transportation companies who perform work in the territories of both Contracting States and who would otherwise be covered under the Laws of both Contracting States shall, with respect to that work, be subject to the Laws of only the Contracting State in the territory of which the company has its headquarters. However, if such employees reside in the territory of the other Contracting State, they shall be subject to the Laws of only that Contracting State.

6.
- (a) This Agreement shall not affect the provisions of the Vienna Convention on Diplomatic Relations of April 18, 1961, or of the Vienna Convention on Consular Relations of April 24, 1963.
- (b) Nationals of one of the Contracting State who are employed by the Government of that Contracting State in the territory of the other Contracting State but who are not exempt from the Laws of the other Contracting State by virtue of the Vienna Conventions mentioned in subparagraph(a) of this paragraph shall be subject to the Laws of only the first Contracting State. For the purpose of this paragraph, government employment includes any work performed for a government agency or instrumentality.

7. At the request of the worker and the employer or self employed person, the Competent Authorities of the two Contracting States may agree to grant an exception to the provisions of this Article with respect to particular persons or categories of persons, provided that any affected person shall be subject to the Laws of one of the Contracting States.

Part III: Provisions on Benefits

Article 7: United States Benefits
1. Where a person has completed at least six·(6) quarters of coverage under United States Laws but does not have sufficient Periods of Coverage to satisfy the requirements for entitlement to Benefits under United States Laws, the Competent Institution of the United States shall take into account, for the purpose of establishing entitlement to Benefits under this Article, Periods of Coverage which are credited under Uruguayan Laws and which do not coincide with Periods of Coverage already credited under United States Laws.
2. Where it is not possible to determine the calendar quarter during which a specific Period of Coverage was completed under the Laws of the United States, the United States Competent Institution will presume that the Period of Coverage does not coincide with a Period of Coverage completed in Uruguay.
3. In determining eligibility for Benefits under paragraph 1 of this Article, the Competent Institution of the United States shall credit one·(1) quarter of coverage for every ninety (90) days of coverage certified by the Competent Institution of Uruguay. The total number of quarters of coverage to be credited for one year shall not exceed four (4).
4. The Competent Institution of the United States shall not take into account Periods of Coverage that occurred prior to the earliest date when Periods of Coverage may be credited under United States

Laws nor will the Competent Institution of the United States take into account any Periods of Coverage that are not based on wages or self-employment income.

5. Where entitlement to a Benefit under United States Laws is established according to the provisions of paragraph 1 of this Article, the Competent Institution of the United States shall compute a pro rata Primacy Insurance Amount in accordance with United States Laws based on:
   a) the person's average earnings, credited exclusively under United States Laws; and
   b) the ratio of the duration of the person's Periods of Coverage completed under United States Laws, to the total duration of a coverage lifetime as determined in accordance with United States Laws.

   Benefits payable under United States Laws shall be based on the pro rata Primary Insurance Amount.

6. Entitlement to a Benefit under United States Laws that results from paragraph 1of this Article shall terminate with the. acquisition of sufficient Periods of Coverage under United States Laws to establish entitlement to an equal or higher Benefit without the need to invoke the provision of paragraph 1 of this Article.

7. Article 4 of this Agreement shall be applied by the United States in a manner consistent with section 233(c)(4) of the United States Social Security Act.

Article 8: Uruguayan Benefits

1. If Periods of Coverage have been completed under the Laws of the two Contracting States, the Uruguayan Competent Institution shall take into account - if necessary - the Periods of Coverage completed under the Laws of the other Contracting State in order to determine the entitlement to the Benefits according to the applicable Laws, provided that the Periods of Coverage do not overlap.

2. To establish the applicability of the provisions on the calculation of total Periods of Coverage and Benefit entitlement under the Uruguayan Laws the periods completed in a third State bound by a Social Security Agreement with Uruguay which provides for the aggregation of Periods of Coverage shall be taken into account if necessary.
3. Benefits shall be provided under the intergenerational solidarity retirement system, and when applicable, the Benefits generated under the system of mandatory individual savings (capitalization) will be added.
4. The Uruguayan Competent Institution shall establish the individual entitlement to a Benefit and shall calculate the Benefits taking into account the Periods of Coverage completed under the Uruguayan Laws, as well as those completed under the United States Laws.
Benefits provided shall result from the most favorable calculation to the beneficiary by one·or the other procedure, regardless of any Benefit determination made by the United States Competent Institution.
5. When totalizing the Periods of Coverage in order to add the Periods of Coverage completed under the Laws of the United States to those completed under the Uruguayan Laws, the Uruguayan Competent Institution shall apply the following calculation rules to establish the amount of Benefits:
    a) The Competent Institution shall determine the amount of the Benefit that the person would·be entitled to, as if all creditable Periods of Coverage had been completed under its Laws (theoretical benefit).
    b) The Competent Institution shall establish the amount of the Benefit by applying to the theoretical Benefit estimated according to its Laws, the same proportion that exists between the creditable Period of Coverage completed under the Uruguayan Laws, and the total creditable Periods of Coverage completed under the Laws of the two Contracting States (pro rata Benefit).

6. Where the Uruguayan Laws require that, in order to be entitled to the Benefit, the Periods of Coverage should be completed in a certain time immediately prior to the event giving rise to the Benefit, this condition will be considered as fulfilled, if the person is contributing under the Laws of the United States and has credit for at least one (1) quarter of coverage under such Laws during the eight (8) calendar·quarters immediately preceding the calendar quarter in which the insured event occurs according to the Laws of Uruguay.

Part IV: Miscellaneous Provisions

Article 9: Administrative Arrangements

The Competent Authorities of the two Contracting States shall:

a) make all necessary administrative arrangements for the implementation of this Agreement and designate Liaison Institutions;
b) communicate to each other information concerning the measures taken for the application of this Agreement; and
c) communicate to each other, as soon as possible, information concerning all changes in their respective Laws which may affect the application of this Agreement.

Article 10: Mutual Assistance

The Competent Authorities and the Competent Institution of the Contracting States; within the scope of their respective authorities, shall assist each other in implementing this Agreement. This assistance shall be free of charge, subject to exceptions to be agreed upon in an administrative arrangement.

Article 11: Confidentiality of Exchanged Personal Data

1. Unless otherwise required by the national statutes of a Contracting State, Personal Data transmitted in accordance with this Agreement to one Contracting State by the other Contracting State shall be used exclusively for purposes of administering this Agreement and the applicable Laws. The receiving Contracting State's national statutes for the protection of privacy and confidentiality of Personal Data and the provisions of this Agreement shall govern such use.
2. The Competent Authorities of the Contracting States shall inform each other about all amendments to their national statutes regarding the protection of privacy and confidentiality of Personal Data that affect the transmission of Personal Data.
3. The Competent Authority or Competent Institution requesting or transmitting Personal Data pursuant to this Agreement, upon request must disclose to a person the following:
   a) the content of his or her Personal Data,
   b) the Competent Institution receiving his or her Personal Data,
   c) the duration of use of his or her Personal Data; and
   d) the purpose and legal grounds for which his or her Personal Data were used or requested.
4. The Competent Authority or Competent Institution transmitting Personal Data pursuant to this Agreement shall take all reasonable steps to ensure that transmitted Personal Data are accurate and limited o data required to fulfill the receiving Competent Authority's or Competent Institution's request. In accordance with their respective national statutes, the receiving Competent Authority or Competent Institution shall correct or delete·any inaccurate transmitted Personal Data and any data not required to fulfill the receiving Competent Institution's request, and immediately notify the other Contracting State's Competent Authority or Competent Institution of such correction. This shall not limit a person's right to request such correction of his or her

Personal Data directly from the Competent Institutions under their respective national statutes.
5. Both the transmitting and the receiving Competent Authority or Competent Institution shall effectively protect Personal Data against unauthorized or illegal access, alteration, or disclosure.

Article 12: Confidentiality of Exchanged Employers Information

Unless otherwise required by the national statutes of a Contracting State, employers' information transmitted between the Contracting States in accordance with this Agreement shall be used exclusively for purposes of administering this Agreement and the applicable Laws. The receiving Contracting State's national statutes tor the protection and confidentiality of employers' information and the provisions of this Agreement shall govern such use.

Article 13: Documents
1. Where the Laws of Contracting State provide that any document which is submitted to the Competent Authority or a Competent Institution of that Contracting State shall be exempted, wholly or partly, from fees or charges, including consular and administrative fees, the exemption shall also apply to corresponding documents which are submitted to the Competent Authority or a Competent Institution of the other Contracting State in the application of this Agreement.
2. Documents and certificates presented for purposes of this Agreement shall be exempted from requirements for authentication by diplomatic or consular authorities, as well as translation, notarization, and registration.
3. Copies of documents certified as true and exact copies by a Competent Institution of one Contracting State shall be accepted as true and exact copies by a Competent Institution of the other Contracting State, without further certification. The Competent Institution of each Contracting State shall be the final judge of the

probative value of the evidence submitted to it from whatever source.

Article 14: Correspondence and Languages

1. The Competent Authorities and Competent Institutions of the Contracting States may correspond directly with each other and with any person, wherever the person may reside, whenever it is necessary for the administration of this Agreement.
2. The Competent Authority or Competent Institution of a Contracting State shall not reject applications or documents solely because they are written in the language of the other Contracting State.

Article 15: Claims

1. A written claim for Benefits filed with a Competent Institution of one Contracting State under its Laws or under this Agreement shall be considered as filed with the Competent Institution of the other Contracting State if the applicant so requests.
2. If an applicant has filed a written claim for Benefits with a Competent Institution of one Contracting State and has not explicitly requested that the claim be restricted to Benefits under the Laws of that Contracting State, the claim shall also protect the rights of claimants under the Laws of the other Contracting State if the applicant provides information at the time of filing indicating that the person on whose record Benefits are claimed has completed Periods of Coverage under the Laws of the other Contracting State.
3. The provisions of Part III of this Agreement shall apply only to Benefits for which a claim is filed on·or after the date on which this Agreement enters into force.

Article 16: Reconsideration, Appeals, and Time Limits

1. A written request for a reconsideration or appeal of a determination made by a Competent Institution of one Contracting State may be validly filed with a Competent Institution of either Contracting State. The reconsideration or appeal shall be decided according to the procedure and Laws of the Contracting State whose decision is being reconsidered or appealed.
2. Any claim, notice or written request for a reconsideration or appeal which, under the Laws of one Contracting State must have been filed within a prescribed period with a Competent Institution of that Contracting State; but which is instead filed within the same period with a Competent Institution of the other Contracting State, shall be considered to have been filed on time.

Article 17: Transmittal of Claims, Notices, Reconsiderations, and Appeals

In any case to which the provisions of Article 15 or 16 or both of this Agreement apply the Competent Institution to which the claim, notice, or written request for a reconsideration or appeal has been submitted shall indicate the date of receipt on the document or any form developed for this purpose in accordance with Article 9 subparagraph (a), and transmit it without delay to the Liaison Institution of the other Contracting State.

Article 18: Currency

1. Payments under this Agreement may be made in the currency of the Contracting State making the payments.
2. In case provisions designed to restrict the exchange or export of currencies are introduced by either Contracting State the Governments of both Contracting States shall immediately take measures necessary to ensure the transfer of sums owed by either Contracting State under this Agreement.

Article 19: Resolution of Disagreements
1. Any disagreement regarding the interpretation or application of this Agreement shall be resolved by consultation between the Competent Authorities.
2. If a disagreement is not resolved within twelve (12) months from the initiation of the consultations in accordance with paragraph 1 of this Article, either Contracting State may request resolution through diplomatic channels, in which case the Contracting States shall seek to resolve the dispute through such channels.

Article 20: Supplementary Agreements
   This Agreement may be amended in the future by supplementary agreements.

Part V: Transitional and Final Provisions

Article 21: Transitional Provisions
1. This Agreement shall not establish any claim to payment of a Benefit for any period before the date of the entry into force of this Agreement, or to a lump-sum death payment if the person died before the entry into force of this Agreement.
2. Except as otherwise provided in this Agreement, in determining the right to Benefits under this Agreement, consideration shall be given to Periods of Coverage completed under the Laws of both Contracting States and other events that occurred before the entry into force of this Agreement.
3. In applying paragraph 1, 2, 3, or 4 of Article 6 of this Agreement in the case of persons who were sent to work in or transferred to the territory of a Contracting State prior to the date of entry into force of this Agreement, the period of employment or self-employment referred to in that paragraph shall be considered to begin on the date of entry into force of this Agreement.

4. Determinations concerning entitlement to Benefits made before the entry into force of this Agreement shall not affect rights arising under it.
5. The application of this Agreement shall not result in any reduction in the amount of a Benefit to which entitlement was established prior to the entry into force of this Agreement

Article 22: Duration
1. This Agreement shall remain in force until the expiration of one (1) calendar year following the year in which written notice of its denunciation is given by one of the Contracting States to the other Contracting State.
2. If this Agreement is terminated by denunciation, rights regarding entitlement to or payment of Benefits acquired under it shall be retained. The Contracting States shall make arrangements dealing with rights in the process of being acquired.

Article 23: Entry into Force
1. Each Contracting State shall transmit to the other Contracting State a diplomatic note of the compliance with all legal and constitutional requirements for the entry into force of this Agreement.
2. This Agreement shall enter into force on the first day of the third month following the date of the last note of an exchange of diplomatic notes in which the Contracting States notify each other of the completion of their respective necessary internal procedures for entry into force of this Agreement.

IN WITNESS WHEREOF, the undersigned, being duly authorized thereto, have signed the present Agreement.

DONE Montevideo on this day of January 2017 in duplicate, in the English and Spanish languages, both texts being equally authentic.

For the United States of America: Kelly Keiderling

For the Oriental Republic of Uruguay: Ernesto Murro

ADMINISTRATIVE ARRANGEMENT BETWEEN THE COMPETENT AUTHORITIES OF THE UNITED STATES OF AMERICA AND THE ORIENTAL REPUBLIC OF URUGUAY FOR THE IMPLEMENTATION OF THE AGREEMENT ON SOCIAL SECURITY BETWEEN THE UNITED STATES OF AMERICA AND THE ORIENTAL REPUBLIC OF URUGUAY

The Competent Authority of the United States of America and the Competent Authority of the Oriental Republic of Uruguay, In conformity with Article 9(a) of the Agreement on Social Security between the United States of America and the Oriental Republic of Uruguay, signed on January 10, 2017, hereinafter referred to as the "Agreement," have agreed as follows:

Chapter I. General Provisions

Article 1

Where terms that appear in the Agreement are used in this Administrative Arrangement, they shall have the same meaning as they have in the Agreement.

Article 2

1) The Liaison Institutions defined in Article 1.1(e) of the Agreement shall be:
    a) for the United States, the Social Security Administration (la Administración de la Seguridad Social); and
    b) for Uruguay, the Banco de Previsión Social (the Social Security Bank).
2) The Liaison Institutions referred to in paragraph 1 of this Article are to decide upon the joint procedures and methods necessary for

the implementation of the Agreement and this Administrative Arrangement.

Chapter II. Provisions on Applicable Laws

Article 3

1) Where the Laws of one Contracting State are applicable in accordance with any of the provisions of Article 5 or 6 of the Agreement, the Liaison Institution of that Contracting State, upon request of the employer or self-employed person, shall issue a certificate stating that the employee or self-employed person is subject to those Laws and indicating the duration for which the certificate shall be valid. This certificate shall be evidence that the employee or self-employed person is exempt from the Laws on compulsory coverage of the other Contracting State.
2) The certificate referred to in paragraph 1 of this Article shall be issued:
   a) in the United States, by the Social Security Administration (la Administración de la Seguridad Social); and
   b) in Uruguay, by the Banco de Previsión Social (the Social Security Bank).
3) The Liaison Institution of a Contracting State that issues a certificate referred to in paragraph 1 of this Article shall furnish a copy of the certificate or mutually decided information from the certificate to the Liaison Institution of the other Contracting State as needed.

Chapter III. Provisions on Benefits

Article 4

1) Claims for Benefits under the Agreement shall be submitted on forms to be developed by the Liaison Institutions of the two Contracting States.
2) The Competent Institution of the Contracting State, with which a claim for Benefits is first filed in accordance with Article 15 of the Agreement, shall provide the Liaison Institution of the other Contracting State with such evidence and other information in its possession as may be required to complete action on the claim.
3) The Competent Institution of a Contracting State which receives a claim that was first filed with a Competent Institution or Liaison Institution of the other Contracting State shall without delay provide the Liaison Institution of the other Contracting State with such evidence and other available information in its possession as may be required for it to complete action on the claim.
4) The Competent Institution of the Contracting State with which a claim for Benefits has been filed shall verify the information pertaining to the claimant and the claimant's family members. The Liaison Institutions of both Contracting States shall decide the types of information to be verified.

Chapter IV. Miscellaneous Provisions

Article 5

1) In accordance with measures to be decided pursuant to paragraph 2 of Article 2 of this Administrative Arrangement, the Liaison Institution of one Contracting State shall, upon request by the Liaison Institution of the other Contracting State, furnish available information relating to the claim of any specified individual for the purpose of administering the Agreement.

2) For the purpose of facilitation of the implementation of the Agreement and this Administrative Arrangement, the Liaison Institutions may decide on measures for the electronic exchange of data.

Article 6

The Liaison Institutions shall exchange statistics on the number of certificates issued under Article 3 of this Administrative Arrangement and on the payments made to beneficiaries under the Agreement. These statistics shall be furnished annually in a manner to be decided by the Liaison Institutions.

Article 7
1) Where assistance is requested and provided under Article 10 of the Agreement, expenses other than regular personnel and operating costs shall be reimbursed to the Competent Institution providing the assistance, except as may be otherwise decided by the Competent Authorities or Liaison Institutions of the Contracting States.
2) Upon request, the Liaison Institution of either Contracting State shall furnish without cost to the Liaison Institution of the other Contracting State any medical information and documentation in its possession to assess the disability of the claimant or beneficiary.
3) Medical examinations of persons who reside in the territory of one of the Contracting States, which are required under the Laws of the other Contracting State, shall be arranged by the Liaison Institution of the first Contracting State, upon the request and at the expense of the requesting Liaison Institution. The costs of medical examinations shall not be refunded if they are performed for the use of the Competent Institutions of both Contracting States.
4) The Liaison Institution of one Contracting State shall reimburse amounts owed under paragraph 1 or 3 of this Article upon

presentation of a statement of expenses by the Liaison Institution of the other Contracting State.

Article 8

This Administrative Arrangement shall enter into force on the date of entry into force of the Agreement and remain in force as long as the Agreement is in force.

DONE at Montevideo, this 10th day of January, 2017, in duplicate in the English and Spanish languages, both texts being equally authentic.

For the Competent Authority of the United States of America:
Kelly Keiderling
For the Competent Authority of the Oriental Republic of Uruguay:
Ernesto Murro

SOCIAL SECURITY MEMORANDUM

Date: March 2, 2017
Refer To: TCC
To: Stephen C. Goss, ASA, MAAA Chief Actuary
From: Chris Chaplain, ASA /s/
Supervisory Actuary
Nettie Barrick /s/
Actuary

Subject: Estimated Effects of a Potential Totalization Agreement between Uruguay and the United States-INFORMATION

This memorandum and the attached tables present estimates of the effects of implementing a potential totalization agreement with Uruguay assuming an effective date of January 1, 2019.

Table 1 shows the estimated net additional program costs to the Social Security systems of the United States (OASDI) and Uruguay under the potential agreement for fiscal years 2019 through 2025. In each case, these net additional program costs arise under the respective systems due to: (I)

benefits payable because of the agreement; and (2) tax contributions eliminated for temporary foreign workers under the agreement.

The first three rows of Table 2 show estimates of the numbers of persons (as of mid-year) who would receive "totalized" benefits from each system. The fourth row of the table shows the number of Urugnayan citizens living outside the U.S., and Uruguayan residents who are citizens of a third country, who would be affected by removing the 5-year U.S. residency requirement for survivor or dependent benefits. The last two rows of the table show estimates of the numbers of temporary foreign workers in the respective countries who would be exempt from taxation by the local Social Security system under a totalization agreement. Under the agreement, U.S. workers working for a U.S. firm in Uruguay for a period expected to last 5 years or less would pay Social Security taxes only to the United States. Uruguayan workers working for a Uruguayan firm in the U.S. for a period expected to last 5 years or less would pay Social Security taxes only to the Uruguayan system. We base estimates shown in the tables on the intermediate set of assumptions of the 2016 OASDI Trustees Report. The exchange rate used in these estimates is 28.275769 Uruguayan pesos (UYU) per U.S. dollar (1 UYU = $0.035366), the exchange rate as of January 25, 2017. To provide a frame of reference, the average exchange rate over the past 5 years is about 24.3695 UYU per U.S. dollar, with a low of about 18.7354 UYU per U.S. dollar and a high of about 32.5773 UYU per U.S. dollar.

These estimates are subject to much uncertainty. Many of the estimates are based on limited data for Uruguay and the assumption that certain relationships that apply on average for other countries where totalization agreements already exist will apply for Uruguay as well.

Numbers of Totalized Beneficiaries

To estimate the numbers of totalized beneficiaries under the U.S. Social Security system resulting from an agreement with Uruguay, we use two data sources for 21 of the existing agreement countries in a regression analysis.[1] From Census Bureau files, we estimate immigration and emigration. From counts of nonimmigrant visas issued by U.S. Foreign Service posts in each country to persons traveling to the U.S., over a 5-year period roughly 30 years ago when 2019-2025 retirees potentially receiving benefits under the totalization agreement were in their prime working years, we estimate the influx of temporary workers. This analysis yields an estimate of about 320 totalized beneficiaries under the U.S. Social Security system at the end of the 5th year of the potential agreement with Uruguay. For 9 of these existing-agreement countries, the predicted number of beneficiaries from the regression is higher than the actual number at the end of 5 years, by a median value of about 82 percent of the actual number. For 12 of these existing-agreement countries, the predicted number of beneficiaries from the regression is lower than the actual number, by a median value of about 29 percent of the actual number. Therefore, the number of OASDI beneficiaries at the end of the 5th year of implementation would be: (1) about 180, if the median relationship for countries with fewer beneficiaries than predicted by the regression analysis applies to Uruguay; and (2) about 450, if the median relationship for countries with more beneficiaries than predicted by the regression applies to Uruguay.

To estimate the number of totalized Uruguayan beneficiaries under the agreement, we use Census Bureau immigration data to make an initial estimate of the number of beneficiaries who will receive totalized benefits under the Uruguayan system. We then adjust this estimate based on a comparison of the number of beneficiaries under the U.S. system estimated using the same data, and the regression estimate for the U.S. system described in the previous paragraph.

Totalization agreements provide OASDI benefits mainly to three groups. The first group is Uruguayan non-immigrants (temporary visa

---

[1] We excluded 4 totalization agreement countries from the analysis-the Slovak Republic and Hungary because the agreements have not been in effect long enough for us to have five full years of data available, South Korea because work before 1986 in South Korea would not be counted as coverage in determining eligibility for totalized benefits, Luxembourg because of lack of data, and Canada because it is a border country with emigrant and immigrant patterns that would likely vary widely from those of Uruguay.

holders) who work in the U.S. for less than 10 years. These workers would have coverage under the U.S. Social Security system (unless they work for a Uruguayan firm in the U.S. for 5 years or less after a totalization agreement becomes effective), and may be eligible for U.S. totalized benefits when their work in Uruguay is also considered. The second group is legal immigrants (generally permanent) from Uruguay to the U.S. who work in the U.S. for less than 10 years, frequently because they immigrate later in their working careers. The third group is emigrants from the U.S. to Uruguay (Uruguay -born or U.S.-born) who worked in the U.S. for less than 10 years, frequently because they emigrated relatively early in their careers.

A totalization agreement between Uruguay and the United States precludes OASDI disability benefits for Uruguayan workers employed by a Uruguayan employer in the U.S. for 5 years or less who become disabled while working in the U.S. or shortly thereafter. However, temporary workers from Uruguay are unlikely to work long enough to qualify for U.S. disability benefits (generally at least 5 years), and are expected to be relatively healthy at the time they come to the U.S. to work. Therefore, we believe that reductions in OASDI disability benefits due to eliminating double taxation under a totalization agreement between Uruguay and the United States would be minimal. Similarly, we believe the reductions in disability benefits under the Uruguayan system would be very small, relative to removing taxation to the Uruguayan system for temporary U.S. workers in Uruguay.

5-Year Residency Requirement

In addition to estimates of the number of persons who would receive totalized OASDI benefits, we also estimate the number of alien dependents and survivors who do not meet the 5-year U.S. residency requirement for receipt of Social Security benefits. These individuals would receive OASDI benefits under a totalization agreement because the residency requirement does not apply to totalization countries.

Effects Related to Other US. Social Insurance Programs

The principal financial effects of a totalization agreement apply to the Social Security programs of the countries involved. Totalization agreements do not cover Medicare benefits. Thus, the U.S. cannot use credits for work in Uruguay to establish entitlement under the Medicare program. However, the tax side of the U.S. Medicare program would be affected because of the removal of double taxation for Uruguayan workers who temporarily work in the U.S. for a Uruguayan firm. We do not expect corresponding reduced Medicare outlays, because attainment of Medicare entitlement by these workers is highly unlikely under the current (no totalization) rules. Medicare eligibility is largely restricted to individuals who either: (I) are at least age 65 and eligible for U.S. Social Security benefits; or (2) were entitled to U.S. Social Security disability benefits (as a disabled worker, disabled widow(er), or disabled adult child) for at least 24 months. Furthermore, Medicare reimbursement is generally restricted to services provided in the U.S. Under the current (no totalization) rules, it is unlikely that temporary workers from Uruguay would {a) work enough to qualify for Medicare and {b) live in the U.S. when they might avail themselves of Medicare services; therefore, we believe a totalization agreement between Uruguay and the United States would reduce Medicare benefits very minimally.

By law, totalization agreements do not affect payroll taxes paid for work injury (workers' compensation) and unemployment programs administered by the United States. Therefore, Uruguayan temporary workers employed by Uruguayan firms in the U.S., and their employers would still be required to pay any applicable workers' compensation and unemployment payroll taxes. These programs generally operate at the state, and not the federal, level.

Effects Related to Other Uruguayan Social Insurance Programs

Under a totalization agreement, the Uruguayan system would no longer require U.S. temporary workers in Uruguay (and their U.S.-based employers) to pay into Uruguay's national health insurance system. The reduction in contributions increases from an estimated $0.9 million in fiscal year (FY) 2019 to $1.6 million in FY 2025. These estimates assume the current contribution rate of 11.5% (5% employer, estimated average 6.5% employee) to the Uruguayan national health insurance system continues through this period. By eliminating contributions to the Uruguayan national health insurance system for these temporary U.S. workers in Uruguay, a totalization agreement would result in these workers no longer being eligible for services under that system. These foregone health insurance services represent a savings to the Uruguayan system.

The value of foregone national health insurance services for U.S. temporary workers in Uruguay is extremely difficult to estimate, but is expected to be small. It is very likely that U.S. temporary workers in Uruguay are relatively healthy and do not need much in the way of health services. Due to the assumed healthiness of the U.S. temporary worker population, the propensity to use health providers outside the Uruguayan system, and the benefits paid by U.S. employers, we estimate, very roughly, that the value of benefits currently provided to U.S. workers by the Uruguayan national health insurance system is about one-tenth of the amount of their contributions to that system. Table 1 shows the estimates of net costs to the Uruguayan health insurance system, which range from $0.8 million in FY 2019 to $1.4 million in FY 2025-about 4 times the estimated net cost to the U.S. Medicare system for those years. For the Uruguayan system, under a totalization agreement, U.S. temporary workers in Uruguay (and their U.S. based employers) would only be relieved of paying retirement, disability, survivor, and health insurance contributions. No other Uruguayan taxes are included in this agreement.

Long-Range Financial Effects

Table 1. Estimated net additional program costs for the U.S. and Uruguayan Social Security (and other) systems under a potential totalization agreement between the two countries, fiscal years 2019-2025 (in millions)

	Fiscal year							
	2019	2020	2021	2022	2023	2024	2025	Total, FY 2019-25
Financial Effects for the U.S. Social Security system:								
Increase in OASDI benefit payments	a	a	$1	$1	$1	$1	$1	$6
Reduction in OASDI tax contributions	$1	$1	1	1	1	1	1	8
Net OASDI cost	1	1	2	2	2	2	3	13
Net cost to the Medicare system	a	a	a	a	a	a	a	2
Net costs to the Social Security System of Uruguay:								
Increase in benefit payments	a	1	1	2	3	3	4	14
Reduction in Uruguayan OASDI tax contributions[b]	a	a	a	1	1	1	1	4
Total	a	1	2	2	3	4	4	17
Net cost to the Uruguayan national health insurance system[c]	1	1	1	1	1	1	1	8

[a] Less than $500,000.

[b] In the absence of a totalization agreement, $2.1 million of the total $3.6 million lost contributions from FY2019- FY2025, would go to a worker's individual account and theoretically be returned to the worker as a retirement or disability benefit, or to the worker's survivors in the event of the worker's death.

[c] Includes health insurance payroll tax contributions that the totalization agreement with Uruguay would eliminate,

Notes:
1. The agreement is assumed to become effective on January 1, 2019.
2. The estimates are based on the intermediate assumptions of the 2016 Trustees Report.
3. Totals may not equal the sums of the components due to rounding.
4. Estimates are in U.S. dollars. The assumed exchange rate is 28 275769 Uruguayan pesos per U.S. dollar.

Social Security Administration
Office of the Chief Actuary
March 2, 2017

Table 2. Estimated number of persons affected by a potential totalization agreement between the United States and Uruguay, fiscal years 2019-2025 (In thousands)

	Fiscal year						
	2019	2020	2021	2022	2023	2024	2025
Number of persons receiving a totalized OASDI benefit based in part on employment in Uruguay (in current-pay status at mid-year)	a	.1	.1	.2	.3	.3	.4
Number of persons receiving a totalized Uruguayan benefit based in part on employment in the United States (in current-pay status at mid-year)	.1	.2	.4	.6	.8	1.0	1.1
Number of persons receiving both a totalized OASDI benefit and a totalized benefit from Uruguay (in current-pay status at mid-year)	a	a	a	a	.1	.1	.1
Number of residents of Uruguay, or Uruguayan citizens living outside the U.S., who would now be able to receive OASDI dependent or survivor benefits because the 5-year residency requirement would no longer apply (in current-pay status at mid-year)	.1	.1	.1	.1	.1	.1	.1
Number of U.S. employees in Uruguay who, along with their employers, would no longer make tax contributions during the year to the Social Security system of Uruguay	.1	.1	.1	.1	.1	.1	.1
Number of Uruguayan employees in the U.S who, along with their employers, would no longer make tax contributions during the year to the OASDHI trust funds	.1	.1	.1	.1	.1	.1	.1

a Fewer than 50.

Notes:
1. The agreement is assumed to become effective on January 1, 2019.
2. The estimates are based on the intermediate assumptions of the 2016 Trustees Report.

Social Security Administration
Office of the Chief Actuary
March 2, 2017

Table 3. Projected Net OASDI Cost of Implementing Proposed Totalization Agreement between U.S. and Uruguay

Year	Additional OASDI Net Benefits For Year[1] (Millions of CPI-Indexed 2016 $)	Change in OASDI Payroll Taxes For Year	Additional OASDI Net Cost For Year[2]	Additional OASDI Net Cost For Year[2] (Millions of $, Present Value as of 1·1-16)	Cumulative OASDI Net Cost For Year[2]
2016	0	0	0	0	0
2017	0	0	0	0	0
2018	0	0	0	0	0
2019	0	-1	1	1	1
2020	0	-1	1	1	2
2021	1	-1	2	1	4
2022	1	-1	2	2	5
2023	1	-1	2	2	7
2024	1	-1	2	2	9
2025	1	-1	2	2	11
2026	1	-1	2	2	13
2027	1	-1	2	2	15
2028	1	-1	2	2	17
2029	1	-1	2	2	19
2030	1	-1	2	2	21
2031	1	-1	2	2	23
2032	1	-1	2	2	25
2033	1	-1	2	2	27
2034	1	-1	2	2	29
2035	1	-1	3	2	30
2036	1	-1	3	2	32
2037	1	-1	3	2	34
2038	1	-1	3	2	36
2039	1	-1	3	2	38
2040	1	·1	3	2	40
2041	1	-1	3	2	41
2042	2	-1	3	2	43
2043	2	-1	3	2	45
2044	2	-1	3	2	47

Table 3. (Continued)

Year	Additional OASDI Net Benefits For Year[1]	Change in OASDI Payroll Taxes For Year	Additional OASDI Net Cost For Year[2]	Additional OASDI Net Cost For Year[2]	Cumulative OASDI Net Cost For Year[2]
	(Millions of CPI-Indexed 2016 $)			(Millions of $, Present Value as of 1·1-16)	
2045	2	-1	3	2	48
2046	2	-1	3	2	50
2047	2	-1	3	2	52
2048	2	-1	3	2	53
2048	2	-2	3	2	55
2050	2	-2	3	2	57
2051	2	-2	3	2	58
2052	2	-2	3	2	so
2053	2	-2	3	2	61
2054	2	-2	4	2	63
2055	2	-2	4	2	65
2056	2	-2	4	2	66
2057	2	-2	4	2	68
2058	2	-2	4	2	69
2059	2	-2	4	2	71
2060	2	-2	4	1	72
2061	2	-2	4	1	74
2062	2	-2	4	1	75
2063	2	-2	4	1	77
2064	2	-2	4	1	78
2065	2	-2	4	1	79
2066	2	-2	4	1	81
2067	2	-2	4	1	82
2068	2	-2	4	1	84
2069	2	-2	5	1	85
2070	3	-2	5	1	86
2071	3	-2	5	1	88
2072	3	-2	5	1	89
2073	3	-2	5	1	90
2074	3	-2	5	1	92
2075	3	-2	5	1	93
2076	3	-2	5	1	94
2077	3	-2	5	1	95
2078	3	-2	5	1	97
2079	3	-2	5	1	98

	Additional OASDI Net Benefits	Change in OASDI Payroll Taxes	Additional OASDI Net Cost	Additional OASDI Net Cost	Cumulative OASDI Net Cost
Year	For Year[1]	For Year	For Year[2]	For Year[2]	For Year[2]
	(Millions of CPI-Indexed 2016 $)			(Millions of $, Present Value as of 1·1-16)	
2080	3	-3	5	1	99
2081	3	-3	8	1	100
2082	3	-3	6	1	102
2083	3	-3	6	1	103
2084	3	-3	6	1	104
2085	3	-3	6	1	105
2086	3	-3	6	1	106
2087	3	-3	6	1	107
2088	3	-3	6	1	109
2089	3	-3	6	1	110
2090	4	-3	6	1	111

Based on Intermediate Assumptions of the 2016 Trustees Report.

[1] Additional benefits less revenue to OASDI from taxes on benefits.

[2] Additional net benefit payments minus change in payroll-tax revenue.

Social Security Administration
Office of the Chief Actuary
March 2, 2017

Implementing the potential totalization agreement between the U.S. and Uruguay would decrease the long-range (75-year) actuarial balance of the OASDI program by an amount that is estimated to be negligible (that is, by less than 0.005 percent of taxable payroll).

Table 3 displays the components of the estimated net cost to the OASDI Trust Funds for years 2016 through 2090 on a "CPI-indexed to 2016" basis, i.e., indexing the amounts back to the year 2016 by assumed changes in the consumer price index (CPI). In addition, the table displays total estimated OASDI net costs on an annual and cumulative present-value basis, i.e., indexing the amounts back to January 1, 2016 by projected interest rates earned by the OASDI Trust Funds on special-issue U.S. Government bonds.

Main Provisions of the United States-Uruguay Social Security Agreement

Introduction

In general, Section 233(c)(l) of the Social Security Act ("Act") requires that international agreements concluded pursuant to that section meet three requirements:

- They must eliminate dual coverage of the same work under the social security systems of the United States and the other agreement country;
- They must allow for combining credits that the worker earns under the two systems for benefit eligibility purposes; and
- When combined credits establish eligibility for U.S. Social Security benefits, the basis for the U.S. benefit payable must be the proportion of the worker's periods of coverage completed under title II of the Act.

The U.S.-Uruguay agreement includes these required provisions.

Elimination of Dual Coverage

The agreement establishes rules to eliminate dual coverage and taxation, the situation that now exists when a person from either the United States or Uruguay works in the other country. The agreement sets forth a general rule under which the social security system of the country where the employee performs the work will cover the employee, subject to the following exceptions:

- If an employer sends an employee from one of the agreement countries to work in the other country for a period not expected to

exceed five years, the agreement provides that the employee will remain covered under the home country's social security system. Under a separate provision of the agreement, this same rule applies to a self-employed person who moves to work in the other country for a period not expected to exceed five years.
- Thus, a person whose U.S. employer temporarily transfers him or her to Uruguay will retain coverage under, and pay contributions to, the U.S. program exclusively. The agreement will relieve the employer and employee (or self-employed person) of the additional burden of paying social security contributions to the Uruguayan program.
- The agreement also sets forth special coverage rules for employees of the governments of the two countries and for workers in international air and maritime transportation.

Totalization Benefit Provisions

The agreement will also help prevent situations where workers suffer a loss of benefit rights because they divide their careers between the United States and Uruguay.

Under the rules that apply to the United States, if a person has:

- credit for at least six quarters of coverage under the U.S. Social Security system; and
- not enough credits under the U.S. Social Security system to qualify for a retirement, survivors, or disability benefit,

The United States will totalize (i.e., combine) the worker's coverage credits from both countries for the purpose of determining eligibility for a U.S. retirement, survivors, or disability benefit. A person is eligible for a benefit if the worker meets the requirements for a benefit under the U.S. Social Security system based on the combined credits. The benefit amount payable to a person who qualifies based on totalized credits is proportional to the amount of coverage completed in the United States.

Under the rules that apply to Uruguay, if a person does not have enough total or recent coverage under the Uruguayan system to qualify for a retirement, survivors, or disability benefit, Uruguay will totalize the worker's coverage credits from both countries for the purpose of determining eligibility for a Uruguayan retirement, survivors, or disability benefit. Where combined credits from both countries establish eligibility, Uruguay will compute a theoretical benefit amount as if the worker had completed his or her U.S. periods of coverage under Uruguayan law. To determine the benefit amount actually payable, Uruguay will prorate the theoretical amount by multiplying it by the ratio of the periods of coverage credited under Uruguayan law to the total periods credited in both countries.

If a person qualifies for a benefit from the social security system of either country without the need to use credits the worker earned under the other country's social security system, a totalized benefit will not be paid by the country under whose laws the person qualifies; rather, a non-totalized benefit will be paid. However, entitlement to such benefit shall not preclude entitlement to a totalized benefit from the social security system of the other country, provided the person meets all the applicable requirements.

UNITED STATES-URUGUAY
ADMINISTRATIVE ARRANGEMENT

Purpose

The administrative arrangement establishes a number of principles which will serve as the basis for developing operating procedures. In particular, it authorizes the designated liaison institutions to develop procedures and forms necessary to implement the principal agreement. The liaison institutions are:

- for the United States, the Social Security Administration (SSA); and
- for Uruguay, the Banco de Prevision Social (BPS).

Elimination of Dual Coverage

The administrative arrangement sets forth rules for issuing the documentation necessary to exempt workers covered under one country's system from coverage under the other country's system. These rules provide that, upon request of a worker, his or her employer, or a self-employed person, the Competent Institution (as defined in the agreement) whose coverage Jaws will apply to a person working in the other country will issue a certificate of coverage. The certificate shall serve as proof of exemption from social security tax obligations under the other country's social security system.

Benefit Provisions

SSA and the Liaison Institution of Uruguay will exchange coverage records and other information required to process benefit claims filed under the agreement. The administrative arrangement sets forth procedures governing this exchange of claims-related information.

PRINCIPAL AGREEMENT: AGREEMENT ON SOCIAL SECURITY BETWEEN THE GOVERNMENT OF THE UNITED STATES OF AMERICA AND THE ORIENTAL REPUBLIC OF URUGUAY

The United States of America ("United States") and The Oriental Republic of Uruguay ("Uruguay") (hereinafter individually known as "Contracting State," or collectively as "Contracting States"), Being desirous of regulating the relationship between the two countries in the field of social security, have agreed as follows:

Part I. General Provisions

Article 1: Definitions[2]

1) For the purposes of this Agreement on Social Security between the United States of America and the Oriental Republic of Uruguay (hereinafter "Agreement"):
    a) "National" means,
        as regards the United States, a national of the United States as defined in Section 101, Immigration and Nationality Act, as amended, and
        as regards Uruguay, a natural or legal citizen as provided for in Articles 73 through 75 of the Constitution of the Republic;[3]

---

[2] Article 1 defines key terms used in this Agreement.
[3] Under section 101(a)(22) of the Immigration and Nationality Act, "the term "national of the United States" means (A) a citizen of the United States, or (B) a person who, though not a citizen of the United States, owes permanent allegiance to the United States." Those in category (B) include natives of American Samoa.
Articles 73 through 75 prescribe categories of persons to whom Uruguayan citizenship is accorded. Natural born citizens include anyone born in the territory of Uruguay and children of Uruguayan citizens regardless of their place of birth, provided they subsequently reside in Uruguay and are recorded in the Civil Register. Naturalized citizens include foreign

b) "Laws" means the laws and regulations specified in Article 2 of this Agreement;[4]
c) "Competent Authority" means,[5]
>as regards the United States, the Commissioner of Social Security, and
>
>as regards Uruguay, the Ministerio de Trabajo y Seguridad Social (Ministry of Labor and Social Security), and by delegation, the Banco de Previsión Social (Social Security Bank);

d) "Competent Institution" means,
>as regards the United States, the Social Security Administration, and
>
>as regards Uruguay, the Banco de Previsión Social (Social Security Bank), the Caja Notarial de Seguridad Social (Notarial Social Security Fund), the Caja de Jubilaciones y Pensiones de Profesionales Universitarios (Pension and Retirement Fund of University Professionals), the Caja de Jubilaciones y Pensiones Bancarias (Banking Pension and Retirement Fund), the Servicio de Retiros y Pensiones Policiales (Police Retirement and Pension Fund), and the Servicio de Retiros y Pensiones de las Fuerzas Armadas (Armed Forces Pension and Retirement Fund);[6]

---

nationals who have capital or own property in the country, are currently employed, and have resided in Uruguay for either 3 years (if they have family in Uruguay) or 5 years (if they have no family in the country). The General Assembly of Uruguay can also naturalize a person on the basis of noteworthy services or outstanding merit.

[4] The term "Laws," as used in this Agreement, refers to each country's social security laws and regulations as set forth in Article 2.

[5] "Competent Authority," wherever it appears in this Agreement, refers to the government official in each country with ultimate responsibility for administering the social security program and the provisions of this Agreement.
The Commissioner of Social Security is the Competent Authority for the United States.
While the Ministerio de Trabajo y Seguridad Social typically holds the position of Competent Authority for issues related to social security in Uruguay, it delegates such authority to the Banco de Prevision Social (BPS) under Uruguay's international agreements program.

[6] "Competent Institution," as used in this Agreement, refers to the administrative body in each country responsible for taking and processing claims and making coverage determinations under each country's social security Laws.

e) "Liaison Institution" means the organization responsible for coordinating and exchanging information between the Competent Institutions of both Contracting States;[7]

f) "Period of Coverage" means a period of payment of contributions or a period of earnings from employment or self-employment, as defined or recognized as a period of coverage by the Laws under which such period has been completed, or any similar period insofar as it is recognized by such Laws as equivalent to a period of coverage;[8]

g) "Benefit" means any benefit provided for in the Laws specified in Article 2 of this Agreement; and [9]

h) "Personal Data" means any information relating to a specific (identified or identifiable) person, as well as any information that can be used to distinguish or trace an individual's identity. This includes, but is not limited to, the following: any individual identifier; citizenship, nationality, statelessness, or refugee status; benefits, eligibility, or other claims information; contact information; medical information or lay information used in a medical determination; information

---

The Social Security Administration (SSA) is the Competent Institution for the United States. However, the U.S. Internal Revenue Service (IRS) retains its responsibility for determining Social Security tax liability based on SSA coverage determinations under this Agreement.

The Competent Institutions designated by Uruguay represent the different types of funds and schemes of social insurance in Uruguay. While the different Competent Institutions each administer individual schemes (for university workers, finance professionals, police, armed services, etc.), the Banco de Prevision Social acts as a liaison between the many different bodies, which each operate under relatively harmonized rules and regulations.

[7] Article 2 of the Administrative Arrangement designates the institutions in each country that will coordinate implementation and administration of this Agreement's coverage and Benefit provisions. SSA is the designated Liaison Institution for the United States. The counterpart Liaison Institution for Uruguay is the BPS.

[8] "Period of Coverage" means any period credited under the social security Laws of either country for purposes of determining Benefit eligibility, including periods of covered employment and self-employment.

[9] "Benefit" refers to old-age, survivors, and disability Benefits provided under the social security Laws of either country. With respect to the United States, the term also includes the lump-sum death payment under section 202(i) of the Social Security Act ("Act"). It also excludes special age-72 payments provided for certain uninsured persons under section 228 of the Act.

Agreement on Social Security between the United States ... 109

about marital, familial, or personal relationships; and information pertaining to work, financial, or economic status.[10]
2. Any term not defined in this Article shall have the meaning assigned to it in the applicable Laws.[11]

Article 2: Material Scope

1. For the purposes of this Agreement, the applicable Laws are:[12]
   a. as regards the United States, the laws governing the Federal old-age, survivors, and disability insurance program:
      (i) Title II of the Social Security Act and regulations pertaining thereto, except sections 226, 226A, and 228 of that title, and regulations pertaining to those sections[13], and
      (ii) Chapters 2 and 21 of the Internal Revenue Code of 1986 and regulations pertaining to those chapters; and[14]
   b. as regards Uruguay, the constitutional, legal and regulatory provisions regarding the contributory benefits for disability, old age and survivors, managed by the Banco de Previsión Social (Social Security Bank), the Caja Notarial de Seguridad Social (Notarial Social Security Fund), the

---

[10] "Personal data" refers to personally identifiable information. Since there is no definition of "personal data" in the Act, this term incorporates and expands upon essential elements of the definition of "information" applying to SSA at 20 CFR 401.25.
[11] If this Agreement does not define a term, that term has the same meaning as it does under each country's national laws.
[12] Article 2.1 specifies the Laws to which this Agreement applies.
[13] For the United States, this Agreement applies to title II of the Act. It also applies to the corresponding tax laws (the Federal Insurance Contributions Act–FICA and the Self-Employment Contributions Act–SECA) and any regulations pertaining to those laws. This Agreement does not apply to Medicare provisions (sections 226 and 226A of the Act). It also does not apply to provisions for special payments to uninsured individuals age 72 or over under section 228 of the Act. Persons to whom this Agreement applies who qualify for Medicare hospital insurance or age-72 payments without application of this Agreement may still receive such benefits.
[14] An employee and his or her employer (or a self-employed person) who are exempt from making U.S. contributions by virtue of Articles 5 and 6 of this Agreement shall be exempt from U.S. FICA and SECA taxes, which include old-age, survivors, disability, and Medicare contributions.

Caja de Jubilaciones y Pensiones de Profesionales Universitarios (Pension and Retirement Fund of University Professionals), the Caja de Jubilaciones y Pensiones Bancarias (Banking Pension and Retirement Fund), the Servicio de Retiros y Pensiones Policiales (Police Retirement and Pension Fund), and the Servicio de Retiros y Pensiones de las Fuerzas Armadas (Armed Forces Pension and Retirement Fund);[15]

2. Unless otherwise provided in this Agreement, the Laws referred to in paragraph 1 of this Article shall not include treaties or other international agreements or supranational legislation on Social Security concluded between one Contracting State and a third State, or Laws promulgated for their specific implementation.[16]

3. This Agreement shall apply to any amendments to the Laws, including changes to the Laws that extend the provisions of this Agreement in a Contracting State to new categories of beneficiaries or new benefits, unless the Competent Authority of such Contracting State notifies the Competent Authority of the other Contracting State in writing within three (3) months after the official publication of the new legislation or regulations that no such extension is intended under the terms of this Agreement.[17]

---

[15] For Uruguay, this Agreement applies to the laws governing Benefits paid on account of old-age, disability, and death under the different schemes currently governing social insurance in Uruguay. An employee and his or her employer (or a self-employed person) who are exempt from making Uruguayan contributions by virtue of Articles 5 and 6 of this Agreement shall be exempt from mandatory pension program and health insurance contributions.

[16] Except as this Agreement itself provides, the Laws to which this Agreement applies do not include treaties and other international agreements. This includes either country's bilateral social security agreements with third countries or multilateral agreements. This provision ensures that if a person has Periods of Coverage in the United States and Uruguay and periods of coverage in a third country with which either country has a social security agreement, SSA cannot combine periods from all three countries to meet U.S. Benefit eligibility requirements.

[17] Article 2.3 provides that this Agreement will automatically apply to any future U.S. or Uruguayan legislation that amends or supplements the Laws set forth in paragraph 1. This includes legislation that creates new categories of beneficiaries or new benefits. The country enacting the legislation may exclude it from the scope of this Agreement by giving written notice to the other country within 3 months of the legislation's official publication.

Article 3: Personal Scope

This Agreement shall apply to[18]:

a) persons who are or have been subject to the Laws of one or both Contracting States; and
b) other persons with respect to the rights they derive from the persons described in sub-paragraph (a) of this Article.

Article 4: Equality of Treatment and Portability of Benefits

1) Unless otherwise provided in this Agreement, persons described in Article 3 of this Agreement who reside in the territory of one Contracting State shall receive equal treatment with Nationals of such Contracting State as regards the application of its Laws.[19]
2) Unless otherwise provided in this Agreement, any provision of the Laws of a Contracting State which restricts entitlement to or payment of Benefits solely because a person resides outside or is absent from the territory of that Contracting State shall not be applicable to a person who resides in the territory of the other Contracting State.[20]

---

[18] Article 3 specifies the persons to whom this Agreement applies. These include persons currently or previously covered under U.S. or Uruguayan Laws. This Agreement also applies to the dependents and survivors of such persons when the Laws of one or both countries confer rights to dependents or survivors because of their relationship to such persons.

[19] Article 4.1 provides that persons to whom this Agreement applies who reside in the United States or Uruguay will receive the same treatment as that country gives its own Nationals. Article 7.7 of this Agreement limits this provision to ensure that any equal treatment accorded in this paragraph does not contravene existing U.S. Laws.

The intent of this provision is to eliminate discrimination based on a person's nationality with respect to Benefits. It would not affect restrictions on Benefit eligibility or payment because a person is not lawfully present in that country or did not have permission to work in that country. The provision also does not affect the coverage provisions of either country's Laws, since Part II of this Agreement deals with social security coverage.

[20] Article 4.2 provides that where the Laws of either country require residence in that country in order to qualify for or receive social security Benefits, a person may also qualify for and receive those Benefits while residing in the other country. By virtue of SSA's published finding about Uruguay's social security system (see FR Doc No 94-7097), the United States has long paid benefits to Uruguayan citizens who do not satisfy U.S. residency requirements for Benefit payment contained in section 202(t)(1) of the Act.

Part II. Provisions Concerning Applicable Laws[21]

Article 5: General Rules[22]

Except as otherwise provided in this Part, a person employed or self-employed within the territory of one of the Contracting States, with respect to that employment or self-employment, shall be subject to the Laws of only that Contracting State.

Article 6: Specific Rules

1) Where a person who is normally employed in the territory of one Contracting State by an employer in that territory is sent by that employer to the territory of the other Contracting State for a temporary period that is not expected to exceed five (5) years, the person shall be subject to the Laws of only the first Contracting State as if the person were still employed in the territory of the first Contracting State.[23]

However, the nonpayment exception is subject to other U.S. payment restrictions based on residency requirements for dependents and survivors; e.g., section 202(t)(11) of the Act. Both countries intend that under this Agreement, Nationals of either country may qualify for or receive Benefits while residing in the other country. Accordingly, under section 233(c)(2) of the Act, this Agreement will permit the United States to pay dependents and survivors currently subject to such residency requirements as well as certain persons who are third country nationals residing in either country.

[21] Part II eliminates dual social security coverage, which occurs when a worker must pay social security taxes to both countries for the same earnings. This Agreement complies with the existing coverage provisions under the Laws of both countries except when necessary to prevent payment of social security taxes to both countries for the same earnings. The provisions in this Part retain the worker's social security coverage and taxation in the country to whose economy he or she has the more direct connection, while exempting the worker from coverage and taxation under the other county's system.

[22] Article 5 establishes a basic territoriality rule, stating that ordinarily, only the country in which a person is working will compulsorily cover the person's work in that country. Work that both countries would otherwise cover will remain covered exclusively under the system of the country where the person is working. Such work activity will be exempt from coverage under the other country's system.

[23] Under Article 6.1, an employee who normally works for an employer located in the United States or in Uruguay who temporarily transfers to work in the other country for the same employer will continue to pay social security taxes to the system of the country from which the employee transferred. This rule will apply only if the employer expects the period of transfer to be 5 years or less.

2) When a self-employed worker transfers from the territory of one Contracting State to the territory of the other Contracting State for the purpose of performing his or her usual work for a period that is not expected to exceed five (5) years, he or she will be exclusively subject to the Laws of the first Contracting State as if he or she continued working in the territory of the first Contracting State.[24]

3) For purposes of applying paragraph 1 of this Article in the case of an employee who is sent from the territory of a Contracting State by an employer in that territory to the other Contracting State to work for an affiliated company of that employer, that employer and the affiliated company of the employer (as defined under the laws of the Contracting State under which the employer is organized) shall be considered one and the same, provided that, if this Agreement did not exist, the employment would have been covered under the Laws of the Contracting State from which the employee was sent.[25]

4) Paragraphs 1 and 3 of this Article shall apply where a person who has been sent by his or her employer from the territory of a Contracting State to the territory of a third State, and who is

---

In determining the length of a transfer for workers whose employer sent them from one country to the other before this Agreement entered into force, both countries will ignore any period of work before this Agreement's entry into force. (See Article 21.3).

[24] Article 6.2 provides that a person who is self-employed in one country who transfers his or her trade or business to the other country for a period of 5 years or less will remain covered only by the country from which he or she moved. This rule will apply only if the self-employed person expects the period of transfer to last 5 years or less.

In determining the duration of such a transfer for a person who moves his or her business to the other country before this Agreement enters into force, Article 21.3 provides that both countries will ignore any period of self-employment before this Agreement's entry into force.

[25] Article 6.3 broadens the scope of Article 6.1 to include certain workers whose employers in one country send them to work for a subsidiary or other affiliate of that employer in the other country.

U.S. Laws allow American companies to extend U.S. Social Security coverage to U.S. citizens and resident aliens employed by an affiliated company in another country. To do this, the parent company in the United States must enter into an agreement with the IRS to pay Social Security contributions on behalf of all U.S. citizens and residents the foreign affiliate employs. Under Article 6.3, U.S. citizens or resident aliens an American employer sends to work for a Uruguayan affiliate for 5 years or less will continue to have coverage in the United States and be exempt from Uruguayan coverage and contributions, if an IRS agreement covers the affiliate.

compulsorily covered under the Laws of that Contracting State while employed in the territory of the third State, is subsequently sent by that employer from the territory of the third State to the territory of the other Contracting State.[26]

5) (a) A person who is employed as an officer or member of a crew on a vessel which flies the flag of one Contracting State and who would be covered under the Laws of both Contracting States shall be subject to the Laws of only the Contracting State whose flag the vessel flies. For purposes of the preceding sentence, a vessel which flies the flag of the United States is one defined as an American vessel under the Laws of the United States.[27]

(b) Traveling employees of air transportation companies who perform work in the territories of both Contracting States and who would otherwise be covered under the Laws of both Contracting States shall, with respect to that work, be subject to the Laws of only the Contracting State in the territory of which the company has its headquarters. However, if such employees reside in the territory of the other Contracting State, they shall be subject to the Laws of only that Contracting State.[28]

---

[26] Under Article 6.4, the provisions of Articles 6.1 and 6.3 will apply even if an employee did not transfer directly from one country to the other, but first transferred to work in a third country.

[27] Article 6.5(a) states that an employee on a U.S. or Uruguayan ship, who would otherwise have coverage in both countries, will have coverage only in the country whose flag the ship flies. U.S. Law considers a ship to fly the flag of the United States if the Act defines it as an American vessel. Section 210(c) of the Act defines an American vessel as one that is, "documented or numbered under the laws of the United States; and includes any vessel which is neither documented or numbered under the laws of the United States nor documented under the laws of any foreign country, if its crew is employed solely by one or more citizens or residents of the United States or corporations organized under the laws of the United States or of any State."

[28] Under Article 6.5(b), a member of the flight crew of an aircraft operating between the United States and Uruguay who would otherwise have coverage in both countries will have coverage only in the country in which the company employing the person has its headquarters. However, if the employee resides in the other country, he or she will only have coverage in that country.

6) (a) This Agreement shall not affect the provisions of the Vienna Convention on Diplomatic Relations of April 18, 1961, or of the Vienna Convention on Consular Relations of April 24, 1963.[29]

(b) Nationals of one of the Contracting States who are employed by the Government of that Contracting State in the territory of the other Contracting State but who are not exempt from the Laws of the other Contracting State by virtue of the Vienna Conventions mentioned in subparagraph (a) of this paragraph shall be subject to the Laws of only the first Contracting State. For the purpose of this paragraph, government employment includes any work performed for a government agency or instrumentality.[30]

7) At the request of the worker and the employer or self-employed person, the Competent Authorities of the two Contracting States may agree to grant an exception to the provisions of this Article with respect to particular persons or categories of persons, provided that any affected person shall be subject to the Laws of one of the Contracting States.[31]

---

[29] Article 6.6(a) specifies that the coverage provisions of this Agreement will not affect the relevant provisions of the Vienna Conventions on Diplomatic and Consular Relations. The Vienna Conventions, to which both the United States and Uruguay are parties, address the application of social security provisions in force in the receiving state to diplomatic agents, members of the administrative and technical staffs, member of consular posts and family members of such staff who form part of their households, the service staffs of the missions, and private servants whom the members of such missions employ.

The Vienna Conventions usually exempt such persons from social security coverage and contributions in the host country with respect to services rendered for the sending state, with certain limited exceptions. Persons who do not enjoy an exemption under the Conventions would be subject to the Laws of the host country and the coverage provisions of this Agreement, including Article 6.6 (b), if applicable.

[30] Under Article 6.6(b), if a U.S. or Uruguayan National works for his or her country's Government in the other country, but the Vienna Conventions do not provide an exemption to this person, the person will be subject only to his or her country's Laws. This provision applies to U.S. Government and Uruguayan Government employees, as well as to persons working for a U.S. Government instrumentality.

[31] Under Article 6.7, upon request of a person and his or her employer, either country may grant an exception to the coverage rules of this Agreement if the other country agrees and the person involved retains coverage in one of the countries. Either country may grant such an exception to an individual worker or to all workers under similar circumstances, e.g., in the same profession or working for the same employer. This provision allows the Competent Authorities to resolve anomalous coverage situations that are unfavorable to workers or to eliminate dual coverage in unforeseen.

Part III. Provisions on Benefits[32]

Article 7: United States Benefits[33]

1) Where a person has completed at least six (6) quarters of coverage under United States Laws, but does not have sufficient Periods of Coverage to satisfy the requirements for entitlement to Benefits under United States Laws, the Competent Institution of the United States shall take into account, for the purpose of establishing entitlement to Benefits under this Article, Periods of Coverage which are credited under Uruguayan Laws and which do not coincide with Periods of Coverage already credited under United States Laws.[34]

2) Where it is not possible to determine the calendar quarter during which a specific Period of Coverage was completed under the Laws of the United States, the United States Competent Institution will presume that the Period of Coverage does not coincide with a Period of Coverage completed in Uruguay.[35]

3) In determining eligibility for Benefits under paragraph 1 of this Article, the Competent Institution of the United States shall credit one (1) quarter of coverage for every ninety (90) days of coverage certified by the Competent Institution of Uruguay. The total

---

[32] Part III establishes the basic rules for determining social security Benefit entitlement when an individual has coverage in both countries. It sets out the rules for determining Benefit amounts when entitlement is possible only with combined work credits. Article 7 deals with the U.S. system, and Article 8 contains rules applicable to the Uruguayan system.

[33] Article 7 contains rules for using combined coverage to determine U.S. Benefit eligibility and amounts.

[34] Under Article 7.1, if a person has at least six U.S. quarters of coverage, but not enough quarters to qualify for U.S. Benefits, SSA will take into account Periods of Coverage that Uruguayan Laws credit, if these periods do not coincide with quarters of coverage that the United States already credited.

[35] Since 1978, SSA has credited quarters of coverage based on a worker's total earnings in a given calendar year. It is not generally possible to determine the period in any given calendar year during which a person worked. Accordingly, where necessary, SSA credits Periods of Coverage within such calendar year in a manner to entitle the worker and his or her dependents or survivors to Benefits (see 20 C.F.R. § 404.1908 (b)(2)).

number of quarters of coverage to be credited for one year shall not exceed four (4).[36]

4) The Competent Institution of the United States shall not take into account Periods of Coverage that occurred prior to the earliest date when Periods of Coverage may be credited under United States Laws, nor will the Competent Institution of the United States take into account any Periods of Coverage that are not based on wages or self-employment income.[37]

5) Where entitlement to a Benefit under United States Laws is established according to the provisions of paragraph 1 of this Article, the Competent Institution of the United States shall

---

[36] Article 7.3 establishes how SSA will convert Periods of Coverage under the Uruguayan system into equivalent periods under the U.S. system. The U.S. system measures Periods of Coverage in terms of calendar quarters while the Uruguayan system measures Periods of Coverage in days, months, and years.

Beginning in 1978, SSA bases quarters of coverage on the amount of a person's annual earnings (e.g., for 2015, $1,220 in earnings equals one quarter of coverage). Under Article 7.3, SSA will credit one quarter of coverage in a calendar year for every 90 days of coverage that the Uruguayan Competent Institution certifies for that year.

SSA will not credit more than 4 quarters of coverage for any calendar year. SSA will also not credit months of coverage under Uruguayan Laws that fall within a calendar quarter that SSA already credited as a U.S. quarter of coverage.

[37] For purposes of entitlement to Benefits under this Agreement, SSA will not consider periods of Uruguayan coverage credited prior to 1937, the earliest date for which U.S. law permits crediting Periods of Coverage. SSA also will not consider deemed Periods of Coverage under the Uruguayan system that are not based on a worker's paid contributions to the Uruguayan system, such as credits awarded to mothers based on child care or bonus credits given to teachers.

compute a pro rata Primary Insurance Amount in accordance with United States Laws based on:[38]

a) the person's average earnings, credited exclusively under United States Laws; and

b) the ratio of the duration of the person's Periods of Coverage completed under United States Laws, to the total duration of a coverage lifetime as determined in accordance with United States Laws.

Benefits payable under United States Laws shall be based on the pro rata Primary Insurance Amount.

6) Entitlement to a Benefit under United States Laws that results from paragraph 1 of this Article shall terminate with the acquisition of sufficient Periods of Coverage under United States Laws to establish entitlement to an equal or higher Benefit without the need to invoke the provision of paragraph 1 of this Article.[39]

7) Article 4 of this Agreement shall be applied by the United States in a manner consistent with section 233(c)(4) of the United States Social Security Act.[40]

---

[38] Article 7.5 describes the method of computing U.S. Benefit amounts when SSA establishes entitlement by totalizing (i.e., combining) U.S. and Uruguayan coverage. Persons whose U.S. coverage alone qualifies them for U.S. Benefits will not receive U.S. totalization Benefits.

Under Article 7.5, the amount of the worker's Benefit depends on both the level of his or her earnings and the duration of his or her U.S. Social Security coverage. SSA regulations (20 CFR 404.1918) describe this computation procedure in detail.

The first step in the procedure is to compute a theoretical Primary Insurance Amount (PIA) as though the worker had spent a full career under U.S. Social Security at the same level of earnings as during his or her actual periods of U.S. covered work. SSA then prorates the theoretical PIA to reflect the proportion of a coverage lifetime completed under the U.S. program. The regulations define a coverage lifetime as the number of years used in determining a worker's average earnings under the regular U.S. national computation method.

[39] Article 7.6 provides that if a worker entitled to a U.S. totalization Benefit acquires additional U.S. coverage that enables the worker to qualify for an equal or higher Benefit based only on his or her U.S. coverage, SSA will pay the regular national law Benefit rather than the totalization Benefit.

[40] Sections 233(c)(1) and (2) of the Act specify certain benefit and coverage provisions which either must be or may be included in U.S. international Social Security agreements. In

Article 8: Uruguayan Benefits
1) If Periods of Coverage have been completed under the Laws of the two Contracting States[41], the Uruguayan Competent Institution

---

addition, section 233(c)(4) permits agreements to contain other unspecified provisions which are not inconsistent with the provisions of title II of the Act. Article 7.7 is intended to make clear that where the only authority for the equality of treatment provisions in Article 4 of this Agreement is section 233(c)(4) of the Act, these provisions will be applied by the United States only to the extent that they do not conflict with other provisions of title II of the Act.

[41] Uruguay pays social security Benefits to people who meet the applicable eligibility standards, including minimum length-of-work and other requirements. Under Article 8, Uruguay will add a person's U.S. coverage to his or her periods of Uruguayan coverage, if necessary, to meet eligibility rules. If the person meets the requirements based on combined U.S. and Uruguayan credits, Uruguay will pay a Benefit in accordance with its Laws (see Article 2.1(b)) on national old-age, disability, and survivors Benefits.

URUGUAYAN SOCIAL SECURITY BENEFITS

GENERAL
The Uruguayan social security system is a three-pillar structure. The first pillar consists of a non-contributory, means-tested social assistance payment for low-income workers, financed through general government revenues. The first pillar is a flat rate, means tested benefit that is adjusted downward as a person's retirement income increases. First pillar Benefits are not included under the scope of this Agreement. The second pillar is a traditional defined benefit system that provides Benefits on the basis of old-age, disability, and death via pay-as-you-go financing. The third pillar is a mandatory, fully funded system invested in individual pension funds (mandatory for all wage earners and self-employed persons in Uruguay who earn more than a statutorily defined threshold). Third pillar benefit amounts vary somewhat according to the performance of the fund in which the employee elects to invest. Article 8.3 of this Agreement permits a person to receive such a Benefit under the third pillar if he or she qualifies for such Benefit.
This Article applies to the second pillar system, which is a work based program that covers all economically active people in Uruguay. Uruguay pays Benefits under the second pillar in amounts that it bases on the worker's average earnings, number of years of contributions, and age of retirement.

OLD-AGE BENEFITS
Retirement age in Uruguay is age 60. The Uruguayan system requires a minimum of 30 years of covered work in Uruguay for entitlement to an old-age Benefit. Certain activities modify this 30 year requirement, including child care (a mother receives 1 year of credit for each child or adopted child in her care, with a maximum of 5) and teaching (teachers are credited with 4 years for each 3 years of services performed). Additional rules apply for more favorable retirement conditions for pilots, miners, and people who work in strenuous conditions. A person may elect to defer receipt of his or her Benefit until age 70, at which point he or she will be eligible for a higher Benefit amount.

DISABILITY BENEFITS
Uruguay pays two types of disability Benefits - total disability Benefits and a temporary allowance for partial disability.

shall take into account -if necessary- the Periods of Coverage completed under the Laws of the other Contracting State in order

In order to receive a total disability Benefit, a person aged 26 or older must have performed at least 2 years of covered work, at least 6 months of which must have occurred in the period immediately preceding the disability onset. The worker must further be completely incapable of any type of work, and cannot be in receipt of a retirement Benefit. If the worker first became disabled under the age of 26, the 2-year minimum contribution period is waived, but the 6-month requirement remains, along with all the other requirements. Further, if a worker's disability onset was directly linked to his or her work activity, both coverage requirements are waived.

The requirements for receipt of the temporary allowance for partial disability are somewhat less stringent. Like the total disability Benefit, a person aged 26 or older must have performed at least 2 years of covered work, at least 6 months of which must have occurred in the period immediately preceding the disability onset, and also cannot be entitled to a retirement Benefit. However, the worker must only be incapable of performing the same work that he or she was performing at the time the disability occurred. The same coverage exemptions for workers under age 26 and workers whose disability is directly connected to his or her work activity apply to this allowance as apply to the total disability Benefit. This allowance is only payable for a maximum period of 3 years.

SURVIVORS' BENEFITS
Under the Uruguayan system, survivors' Benefits are available to widow(er)s, unmarried children under age 21, children of the worker who were disabled prior to age 21, divorced spouses entitled to alimony at the time of the worker's death, registered partners in a consensual union, and disabled parents of the worker who were dependent on the worker at the time of his or her death. In order for any survivors to be eligible for a Benefit, the deceased must have been working, receiving, or eligible to receive an old-age or disability Benefit or sickness, maternity, work injury, or unemployment benefits (or have died within the 12-month period after unemployment benefits terminated). While Benefits for most children terminate upon attainment of 21 years of age, children who were disabled prior to age 21 can continue to receive Benefits so long as they remain unmarried and disabled. Benefits terminate upon the marriage of any entitled surviving spouse or child.
Survivors' Benefit amounts are based on the amount of the Benefit the worker was receiving, or would have been entitled to, at the time of his or her death. Category I survivors include widows and children, who are entitled to receive 75% of this amount. Category II beneficiaries, including widowers, registered partners, and divorced spouses, are entitled to receive 66% of this amount. Disabled parents of the worker are entitled to receive 50% of this amount.
If there is only one Category I survivor entitled on the worker's record, his or her share is 75%. However, if there is more than one Category I survivor entitled to a Benefit, all survivors split 70% equally, except those with children in care, who get a 14% increase. If there is only one Category II survivor beneficiary, his or her share is 66%. However, if there is more than one Category II survivor entitled to a Benefit, all survivors split 60% equally. In all other cases, the Benefit is split equally among other eligible survivors.

COST-OF-LIVING ADJUSTMENTS
Uruguay provides cost of living adjustments on an annual basis. Benefits increase according to increases in the average wage index for the prior year. This adjustment generally occurs at the beginning of the year, when the prior year's average wage statistics are published.

to determine the entitlement to the Benefits according to the applicable Laws, provided that the Periods of Coverage do not overlap.[42]

2) To establish the applicability of the provisions on the calculation of total Periods of Coverage and Benefit entitlement under the Uruguayan Laws, the periods completed in a third State bound by a Social Security Agreement with Uruguay which provides for the aggregation of Periods of Coverage shall be taken into account if necessary.[43]

3) Benefits shall be provided under the intergenerational solidarity retirement system, and when applicable, the Benefits generated under the system of mandatory individual savings (capitalization) will be added. [44]

4) The Uruguayan Competent Institution shall establish the individual entitlement to a Benefit and shall calculate the Benefits taking into account the Periods of Coverage completed under the Uruguayan Laws, as well as those completed under the United States Laws. Benefits provided shall result from the most favorable calculation to the beneficiary by one or the other procedure, regardless of any

---

[42] Article 8 contains rules for determining Uruguayan Benefit eligibility and amounts for people who have periods of social security coverage in both countries, but who do not have enough Uruguayan coverage to qualify for Uruguayan benefits.
Under Article 8.1, BPS will take U.S. Periods of Coverage into account under this Agreement if the worker has Periods of Coverage in both countries, but not enough Periods of Coverage to qualify for a Benefit by considering only Uruguayan Periods of Coverage. As in the parallel U.S. provision found in Article 7.1 of this Agreement, Uruguay will not count any U.S. Periods of Coverage which coincide with a Period of Coverage already credited under Uruguayan Laws.

[43] Article 8.2 provides that, if a person does not have enough coverage in the United States and Uruguay to receive a Benefit under this Agreement, Uruguay will consider for purposes of entitlement to a Benefit periods of coverage completed in other countries with which it has social security agreements in force.
U.S. Laws only permit the United States to totalize Periods of Coverage on a bilateral basis. Accordingly, Article 2.2 of this Agreement exempts SSA from considering periods of coverage completed under the social security systems of third countries with which it has concluded an agreement for purposes of entitlement to a Benefit under this Agreement.

[44] This provision stipulates that any Benefit paid by Uruguay under this Agreement will be paid under the defined benefit (second pillar) scheme. If the person also made sufficient contributions into mandatory individual savings (third pillar), Uruguay will also pay a corresponding supplemental amount to the basic Benefit.

Benefit determination made by the United States Competent Institution.[45]

5) When totalizing the Periods of Coverage in order to add the Periods of Coverage completed under the Laws of the United States to those completed under the Uruguayan Laws, the Uruguayan Competent Institution shall apply the following calculation rules to establish the amount of Benefits:

   a) The Competent Institution shall determine the amount of the Benefit that the person would be entitled to, as if all creditable Periods of Coverage had been completed under its Laws (theoretical benefit).

   b) The Competent Institution shall establish the amount of the Benefit by applying to the theoretical Benefit estimated according to its Laws, the same proportion that exists between the creditable Period of Coverage completed under the Uruguayan Laws, and the total creditable Periods of Coverage completed under the Laws of the two Contracting States (pro rata Benefit).[46]

6) Where the Uruguayan Laws require that, in order to be entitled to the Benefit, the Periods of Coverage should be completed in a certain time immediately prior to the event giving rise to the Benefit, this condition will be considered as fulfilled, if the person is contributing under the Laws of the United States and has credit for at least one (1) quarter of coverage under such Laws during the

---

[45] Article 8.4 provides that in addition to determining a person's entitlement to Benefits using combined coverage under this Agreement, BPS will also calculate the amount of the Benefit by taking into consideration Periods of Coverage completed in the United States.
Uruguay will pay Benefits under this Agreement according to the manner provided for in its Laws that is most favorable to the beneficiary.

[46] Article 8.5 describes the method by which Uruguay will calculate Benefits payable under this Agreement. BPS will perform two separate Benefit calculations. Initially, it will compute a theoretical Benefit amount as if the worker's U.S. Periods of Coverage had been completed under Uruguayan Laws. BPS will then determine a pro rata Benefit amount by multiplying the theoretical amount described in Article 8.5 (a) by the ratio of the Periods of Coverage completed under Uruguayan Laws to the total Periods of Coverage completed in both countries.
Uruguay will pay Benefits under this Agreement according to the manner provided for in its Laws that is most favorable to the beneficiary.

eight (8) calendar quarters immediately preceding the calendar quarter in which the insured event occurs according to the Laws of Uruguay.[47]

Part IV. Miscellaneous Provisions

Article 9: Administrative Arrangements[48]
The Competent Authorities of the two Contracting States shall:

a) make all necessary administrative arrangements for the implementation of this Agreement and designate Liaison Institutions;
b) communicate to each other information concerning the measures taken for the application of this Agreement; and
c) communicate to each other, as soon as possible, information concerning all changes in their respective Laws which may affect the application of this Agreement.

Article 10: Mutual Assistance
The Competent Authorities and the Competent Institutions of the Contracting States, within the scope of their respective authorities, shall assist each other in implementing this Agreement. This assistance shall be

---

[47] In order to be entitled to certain categories of disability Benefits under Uruguayan Laws, a worker must have earned Periods of Coverage in a six-month period immediately prior to the onset of his or her disability. Under Article 8.6, work that was covered under U.S. Laws will count towards this requirement. If the worker has at least 1 U.S quarter of coverage in the 8-quarter period immediately preceding disability onset, he or she will be deemed to meet this decency requirement of Uruguayan Laws.

[48] Article 9 outlines various duties of the Competent Authorities under this Agreement. Paragraph (a) authorizes and requires the Competent Authorities to conclude an Administrative Arrangement and designate Liaison Institutions to facilitate the implementation of this Agreement. Paragraph (b) requires them to notify each other of steps they take unilaterally to implement this Agreement. Paragraph (c) obligates the Competent Authorities to notify each other of any changes in their social security Laws that may affect the application of this Agreement.

free of charge, subject to exceptions to be agreed upon in an administrative arrangement.[49]

Article 11: Confidentiality of Exchanged Personal Data
1) Unless otherwise required by the national statutes of a Contracting State, Personal Data transmitted in accordance with this Agreement to one Contracting State by the other Contracting State shall be used exclusively for purposes of administering this Agreement and the applicable Laws. The receiving Contracting State's national statutes for the protection of privacy and confidentiality of Personal Data and the provisions of this Agreement shall govern such use.[50]
2) The Competent Authorities of the Contracting States shall inform each other about all amendments to their national statutes regarding the protection of privacy and confidentiality of Personal Data that affect the transmission of Personal Data.[51]

---

[49] Article 10 authorizes the two countries to furnish each other non reimbursable assistance in administering this Agreement. Such assistance may include taking Benefit applications and the gathering and exchange, including the electronic exchange, of information relevant to claims filed and Benefits paid under this Agreement. Although Article 10 establishes a general principle that mutual administrative assistance will be free of charge, the provision authorizes the two sides to agree to exceptions, such as the exception for medical examinations in Article 7.3 of the Administrative Arrangement.

[50] Both the United States and Uruguay recognize the great importance of ensuring the integrity of Personal Data, as well as a person's rights pertaining thereto. Accordingly, both countries have statutes and regulations that govern disclosure and provide strict safeguards for maintaining the confidentiality of Personal Data in the possession of their respective governments.
In the United States, these statutes include the Freedom of Information Act, the Privacy Act, section 6103 of the Internal Revenue Code, and pertinent provisions of the Act and other related statutes. In Uruguay, the applicable laws include Law No. 18.331, along with Decree No. 414/009. Article 11.1 provides that both countries will protect Personal Data furnished under this Agreement in accordance with the applicable provisions of the privacy and confidentiality laws of the country that receives the Personal Data.

[51] Article 11.2 provides that if either country modifies any of its statutes that regulate the privacy or confidentiality of Personal Data transmitted between the countries, the Competent Authority of the Contracting State that modified its statute must notify the Competent Authority of the other Contracting State.

3) The Competent Authority or Competent Institution requesting or transmitting Personal Data pursuant to this Agreement, upon request, must disclose to a person the following:[52]
   a) the content of his or her Personal Data,
   b) the Competent Institution receiving his or her Personal Data,
   c) the duration of use of his or her Personal Data, and
   d) the purpose and legal grounds for which his or her Personal Data were used or requested.
4) The Competent Authority or Competent Institution transmitting Personal Data pursuant to this Agreement shall take all reasonable steps to ensure that transmitted Personal Data are accurate and limited to data required to fulfill the receiving Competent Authority's or Competent Institution's request. In accordance with their respective national statutes, the receiving Competent Authority or Competent Institution shall correct or delete any inaccurate transmitted Personal Data and any data not required to fulfill the receiving Competent Institution's request, and immediately notify the other Contracting State's Competent Authority or Competent Institution of such correction. This shall not limit a person's right to request such correction of his or her Personal Data directly from the Competent Institutions under their respective national statutes.[53]

---

[52] Article 11.3 protects a person's right to request particular information about any of his or her Personal Data requested from or transmitted to either country under this Agreement. Article 11.3 also provides that when a person requests such information about his or her Personal Data from a country, that country must provide the requested information to the person.

[53] Article 11.4 provides that both countries will take reasonable steps to ensure the accuracy of Personal Data transmitted between the two countries and will limit the transmission of Personal Data to only that information necessary to satisfy the other country's request. However, if one country later discovers that it transmitted or received inaccurate or outdated Personal Data, or Personal Data not required to satisfy a country's request, the country that discovers the discrepancy will correct or delete the Personal Data in question and immediately notify the Competent Institution of the other country. The countries will perform such correction or deletion in accordance with their respective statutes governing alteration and destruction of data.
Article 11.4 also recognizes the right of a person to ask either Competent Institution directly to correct or delete any of his or her own Personal Data that he or she discovers to be inaccurate or not required to satisfy a Contracting State's request.

5) Both the transmitting and the receiving Competent Authority or Competent Institution shall effectively protect Personal Data against unauthorized or illegal access, alteration, or disclosure.[54]

Article 12: Confidentiality of Exchanged Employers' Information

Unless otherwise required by the national statutes of a Contracting State, employers' information transmitted between the Contracting States in accordance with this Agreement shall be used exclusively for purposes of administering this Agreement and the applicable Laws. The receiving Contracting State's national statutes for the protection and confidentiality of employers' information and the provisions of this Agreement shall govern such use.[55]

Article 13: Documents

1) Where the Laws of a Contracting State provide that any document which is submitted to the Competent Authority or a Competent Institution of that Contracting State shall be exempted, wholly or partly, from fees or charges, including consular and administrative fees, the exemption shall also apply to corresponding documents which are submitted to the Competent Authority or a Competent Institution of the other Contracting State in the application of this Agreement.[56]

---

[54] Both the United States and Uruguay agree to protect the integrity, privacy, and confidentiality of Personal Data under their respective laws when receiving or transmitting such data under this Agreement.

[55] Article 12 provides protections for employers' confidential information. It provides to any business-related information exchanged under this Agreement similar protections to those provided for Personal Data under Article 11 of this Agreement and under each country's national statutes.

[56] Article 13.1 states that if the Laws of one country exempt documents submitted in connection with a social security claim from fees or charges, that exemption will also apply if a country sends such documents to the other country by or on behalf of a claimant or beneficiary.

2) Documents and certificates presented for purposes of this Agreement shall be exempted from requirements for authentication by diplomatic or consular authorities, as well as translation, notarization, and registration.[57]
3) Copies of documents certified as true and exact copies by a Competent Institution of one Contracting State shall be accepted as true and exact copies by a Competent Institution of the other Contracting State, without further certification. The Competent Institution of each Contracting State shall be the final judge of the probative value of the evidence submitted to it from whatever source.[58]

Article 14: Correspondence and Languages

1) The Competent Authorities and Competent Institutions of the Contracting States may correspond directly with each other and with any person, wherever the person may reside, whenever it is necessary for the administration of this Agreement.[59]
2) The Competent Authority or Competent Institution of a Contracting State shall not reject applications or documents solely

---

[57] Some countries require that a diplomatic, consular, or other official representative in the other country certify the authenticity of documents submitted to their social security authorities by or on behalf of persons in another country. Both the United States and Uruguay are parties to the Hague Convention Abolishing the Requirement for Legalisation for Foreign Public Documents. Article 13.2 reaffirms that neither country will require such authentication of documents submitted under this Agreement.

[58] If the Competent Institution of one country certifies that a copy of a document it furnishes to the Competent Institution of the other country is a true and exact copy of an original document, the other country will accept this certification. Nevertheless, each country will remain the final judge of the probative value of any documents submitted to it under this Agreement.

[59] Article 14.1 authorizes direct correspondence between the Competent Authorities and Competent Institutions of the two countries and between these bodies and any person with whom they may need to communicate..

because they are written in the language of the other Contracting State.[60]

Article 15: Claims[61]

1) A written claim for Benefits filed with a Competent Institution of one Contracting State under its Laws or under this Agreement shall be considered as filed with the Competent Institution of the other Contracting State if the applicant so requests.[62]

2) If an applicant has filed a written claim for Benefits with a Competent Institution of one Contracting State and has not explicitly requested that the claim be restricted to Benefits under the Laws of that Contracting State, the claim shall also protect the rights of claimants under the Laws of the other Contracting State if the applicant provides information at the time of filing indicating that the person on whose record Benefits are claimed has completed Periods of Coverage under the Laws of the other Contracting State.[63]

The provisions of Part III of this Agreement shall apply only to Benefits for which a claim is filed on or after the date on which this Agreement enters into force.[64]

---

[60] The Competent Authorities and Competent Institutions of each country may not reject an application or document because it is in the language of the other country. SSA already accepts applications and documents written in any language.

[61] Article 15 provides for situations in which a claim filed for Benefits from one country will also be a claim for Benefits from the other country.

[62] Under Article 15.1, a written claim submitted to the Competent Institution of one country that expresses intent to file for Benefits in the other country will protect the claimants' right to Benefits under the Laws of the other country as if the applicant presented it to the other country, provided the applicant expresses an intent to file for Benefits in the other country when filing the application.

[63] An applicant who files a claim with the Competent Institution of one country may not always know about his or her Benefit rights in the other country. Article 15.2 provides that even if it states no intention to file for Benefits in the other country, a claim will also protect the claimants' rights under the other country's laws if the applicant indicates at the time of filing that the worker had coverage in the other country.

[64] Article 15.3 requires that a person claiming Benefits under this Agreement file a claim on or after the date this Agreement enters into force.

Article 16: Reconsideration, Appeals, and Time Limits

1) A written request for a reconsideration or appeal of a determination made by a Competent Institution of one Contracting State may be validly filed with a Competent Institution of either Contracting State. The reconsideration or appeal shall be decided according to the procedure and Laws of the Contracting State whose decision is being reconsidered or appealed.[65]

2) Any claim, notice or written request for a reconsideration or appeal which, under the Laws of one Contracting State, must have been filed within a prescribed period with a Competent Institution of that Contracting State, but which is instead filed within the same period with a Competent Institution of the other Contracting State, shall be considered to have been filed on time.[66]

Article 17: Transmittal of Claims, Notices, Reconsiderations, and Appeals

In any case to which the provisions of Article 15 or 16, or both, of this Agreement apply, the Competent Institution to which the claim, notice, or written request for a reconsideration or appeal has been submitted shall indicate the date of receipt on the document or any form developed for this purpose in accordance with Article 9 subparagraph (a), and transmit it without delay to the Liaison Institution of the other Contracting State.[67]

---

[65] Both the United States and Uruguay have formal procedures for appealing the determinations of their Competent Institutions. Under Article 16.1, a claimant may file a written appeal of a decision by the Competent Institution of one country with the Competent Institution of either country. The appropriate Competent Institution of the country whose decision a person is appealing will consider the appeal under its own Laws and procedures.

[66] Article 16.2 provides that when the Laws of one country require the submission of a claim, notice, or written appeal within a set time limit, the Competent Institution of that country will consider it filed on time if the claimant files it with the Competent Institution of the other country within that prescribed time limit.

[67] The Competent Institution with which an applicant files a claim, notice, reconsideration, or written appeal under Article 15 or 16 of this Agreement shall transmit it immediately to the Liaison Institution of the other country. The sending Competent Institution will indicate the date on which it received the document.

Article 18: Currency

1) Payments under this Agreement may be made in the currency of the Contracting State making the payments.[68]
2) In case provisions designed to restrict the exchange or export of currencies are introduced by either Contracting State, the Governments of both Contracting States shall immediately take measures necessary to ensure the transfer of sums owed by either Contracting State under this Agreement.[69]

Article 19: Resolution of Disagreements

1) Any disagreement regarding the interpretation or application of this Agreement shall be resolved by consultation between the Competent Authorities.[70]
2) If a disagreement is not resolved within twelve (12) months from the initiation of the consultations in accordance with paragraph 1 of this Article, either Contracting State may request resolution through diplomatic channels, in which case the Contracting States shall seek to resolve the dispute through such channels.[71]

Article 20: Supplementary Agreements[72]

This Agreement may be amended in the future by supplementary agreements.

---

[68] The Competent Institutions may pay Benefits under this Agreement in the currency of either country. The United States pays Benefits abroad in U.S. dollars or, where possible, in local currency. Uruguay pays Benefits abroad in U.S. dollars.
[69] Should either country restrict the exchange of its currency, both Contracting States will take steps to ensure the payment of amounts due under this Agreement.
[70] Article 19.1 requires the Competent Authorities to attempt to resolve any dispute between them regarding this Agreement through consultation or negotiation.
[71] Under Article 19.2, either country can request resolution through diplomatic channels if a dispute cannot be resolved in a 12-month period after consultations commence.
[72] Article 20 provides that future supplementary agreements may amend this Agreement.

Part V. Transitional and Final Provisions

Article 21: Transitional Provisions

1) This Agreement shall not establish any claim to payment of a Benefit for any period before the date of the entry into force of this Agreement, or to a lump-sum death payment if the person died before the entry into force of this Agreement.[73]
2) Except as otherwise provided in this Agreement, in determining the right to Benefits under this Agreement, consideration shall be given to Periods of Coverage completed under the Laws of both Contracting States and other events that occurred before the entry into force of this Agreement.[74]
3) In applying paragraph 1, 2, 3, or 4 of Article 6 of this Agreement in the case of persons who were sent to work in or transferred to the territory of a Contracting State prior to the date of entry into force of this Agreement, the period of employment or self-employment referred to in that paragraph shall be considered to begin on the date of entry into force of this Agreement.[75]

---

[73] The Competent Institutions will pay Benefits based on this Agreement no earlier than the effective date of this Agreement. In addition, no person will be eligible to receive a lump-sum death payment if the worker died prior to the entry into force of this Agreement.

[74] In determining Benefit eligibility and amounts under this Agreement, Article 21.2 provides that the Competent Institutions will consider Periods of Coverage earned before this Agreement enters into force. The Competent Institutions will also consider events relevant to the determination of Benefit rights, such as marriage, death, disability, or attainment of a certain age, which happened prior to this Agreement's effective date.
However, the United States will not consider Uruguayan Periods of Coverage credited prior to 1937, the earliest date for which U.S. Laws permit crediting Periods of Coverage. (See Article 7.4). Additionally, the United States will not pay a lump sum death payment under this Agreement if the person on whose record a claimant files for Benefits died prior to this Agreement's entry into force. (See Article 21.1).

[75] Article 21.3 provides that the Competent Institutions will measure the 5-year period to which paragraphs 1, 2, 3, and 4 of Article 6 refer beginning no earlier than the date this Agreement enters into force. Thus, for persons to whom these provisions apply who were working in the other country before this Agreement's effective date, the prior period will not count for purposes of the 5-year limit.

4) Determinations concerning entitlement to Benefits made before the entry into force of this Agreement shall not affect rights arising under it.[76]

5) The application of this Agreement shall not result in any reduction in the amount of a Benefit to which entitlement was established prior to the entry into force of this Agreement.[77]

Article 22: Duration

1) This Agreement shall remain in force until the expiration of one (1) calendar year following the year in which written notice of its denunciation is given by one of the Contracting States to the other Contracting State.[78]

2) If this Agreement is terminated by denunciation, rights regarding entitlement to or payment of Benefits acquired under it shall be retained. The Contracting States shall make arrangements dealing with rights in the process of being acquired.[79]

Article 23: Entry into Force

1) Each Contracting State shall transmit to the other Contracting State a diplomatic note of the compliance with all legal and constitutional requirements for the entry into force of this Agreement.[80]

---

[76] A decision to award or deny a claim either Competent Institution renders prior to the effective date of this Agreement will not prevent a person from filing a new application for other Benefits that may be payable because of this Agreement.

[77] Article 21.5 guarantees that the entry into force of this Agreement will not result in a reduction in Benefits already payable at the time this Agreement becomes effective.

[78] Either country can terminate this Agreement by giving written notice of denunciation to the other. If either country takes actions to denounce this Agreement, it will remain in effect until the expiration of 1 calendar year after the year in which one of the countries receives written notice of denunciation from the other.

[79] If either country denounces this Agreement, a person will retain Benefit rights acquired before its denunciation. Special arrangements would dictate the extent to which each country would recognize Benefit rights in the process of being acquired at the time of denunciation-for example, Periods of Coverage that had not yet resulted in fully insured status.

[80] Once each country completes its internal approval process, the two governments will exchange formal instruments of approval.

2) This Agreement shall enter into force on the first day of the third month following the date of the last note of an exchange of diplomatic notes in which the Contracting States notify each other of the completion of their respective necessary internal procedures for entry into force of this Agreement.[81]

IN WITNESS WHEREOF, the undersigned, being duly authorized thereto, have signed the present Agreement.

DONE at Montevideo on this 10th day of January, 2017, in duplicate, in the English and Spanish languages, both texts being equally authentic.

For the Government of the United States of America: Kelly Keiderling
For the Oriental Republic of Uruguay: Ernesto Murro

ADMINISTRATIVE ARRANGEMENT BETWEEN THE COMPETENT AUTHORITIES OF THE UNITED STATES OF AMERICA AND THE ORIENTAL REPUBLIC OF URUGUAY FOR THE IMPLEMENTATION OF THE AGREEMENT ON SOCIAL SECURITY BETWEEN THE UNITED STATES OF AMERICA AND THE ORIENTAL REPUBLIC OF URUGUAY

The Competent Authority of the United States of America and the Competent Authority of the Oriental Republic of Uruguay, In conformity with Article 9(a) of the Agreement on Social Security between the United States of America and the Oriental Republic of Uruguay, signed on

---

[81] This Agreement will enter into force on the first day of the third calendar month after the month in which each government receives notification of approval from the other government pursuant to Article 23.1 of this Agreement.

January 10, 2017, hereinafter referred to as the "Agreement," have agreed as follows:

Chapter I. General Provisions

Article 1

Where terms that appear in the Agreement are used in this Administrative Arrangement, they shall have the same meaning as they have in the Agreement.[82]

Article 2
1) The Liaison Institutions defined in Article 1.1(e) of the Agreement shall be: [83]
   a) for the United States, the Social Security Administration (la Administración de la Seguridad Social); and
   b) for Uruguay, the Banco de Previsión Social (the Social Security Bank).
2) The Liaison Institutions referred to in paragraph 1 of this Article are to decide upon the joint procedures and methods necessary for the implementation of the Agreement and this Administrative Arrangement.[84]

---

[82] Article 1 provides that terms have the same meaning in this Administrative Arrangement as they do in the Agreement.
[83] Article 2.1 designates the Liaison Institutions in each country responsible for implementing and administering the coverage and Benefit provisions of the Agreement. The United States designates the Social Security Administration (SSA) as its Liaison Institution, and Uruguay designates the Banco de Previsión Social (BPS) as its counterpart Liaison Institution.
[84] Article 2.2 authorizes and requires the Liaison Institutions of both countries to agree upon those procedures and methods they will use for the implementation of the Agreement and this Administrative Arrangement.

Chapter II. Provisions on Applicable Laws

Article 3

1) Where the Laws of one Contracting State are applicable in accordance with any of the provisions of Article 5 or 6 of the Agreement, the Liaison Institution of that Contracting State, upon request of the employer or self-employed person, shall issue a certificate stating that the employee or self-employed person is subject to those Laws and indicating the duration for which the certificate shall be valid. This certificate shall be evidence that the employee or self-employed person is exempt from the Laws on compulsory coverage of the other Contracting State.[85]
2) The certificate referred to in paragraph 1 of this Article shall be issued:[86]
    a) in the United States, by the Social Security Administration (la Administración de la Seguridad Social); and
    b) in Uruguay, by the Banco de Previsión Social (the Social Security Bank).
3) The Liaison Institution of a Contracting State that issues a certificate referred to in paragraph 1 of this Article shall furnish a copy of the certificate or mutually decided information from the certificate to the Liaison Institution of the other Contracting State as needed.[87]

---

[85] Under Article 3.1, the Liaison Institution of the country whose social security coverage Laws will continue to apply to a person in accordance with the rules in Part II of the Agreement will issue a certificate to that effect when an employer or a self employed person requests one. Employers and self-employed persons should request certificates before work begins in the other country, whenever possible. The certificate will serve as evidence of the exemption of the person from the coverage Laws of the other country when provided to the Liaison Institution of the other country.

[86] SSA (United States) and BPS (Uruguay) will issue coverage certificates.

[87] Article 3.3 provides that the Liaison Institution issuing a coverage certificate will furnish a copy of the certificate or information from the certificate to the Liaison Institution in the other country when needed.

Chapter III. Provisions on Benefits

Article 4
1) Claims for Benefits under the Agreement shall be submitted on forms to be developed by the Liaison Institutions of the two Contracting States.[88]
2) The Competent Institution of the Contracting State, with which a claim for Benefits is first filed in accordance with Article 15 of the Agreement, shall provide the Liaison Institution of the other Contracting State with such evidence and other information in its possession as may be required to complete action on the claim.[89]
3) The Competent Institution of a Contracting State which receives a claim that was first filed with a Competent Institution or Liaison Institution of the other Contracting State shall without delay provide the Liaison Institution of the other Contracting State with such evidence and other available information in its possession as may be required for it to complete action on the claim.
4) The Competent Institution of the Contracting State with which a claim for Benefits has been filed shall verify the information pertaining to the claimant and the claimant's family members. The Liaison Institutions of both Contracting States shall decide the types of information to be verified.[90]

---

[88] The U.S. and Uruguayan Liaison Institutions will agree on special application forms that people who wish to file for Benefits based on the Agreement will use.

[89] Articles 4.2 and 4.3 outline the procedures both countries will follow for the exchange of evidence and information they need to process claims filed under the Agreement.

[90] Article 4.4 deals with the verification of claims information. Both U.S. and Uruguayan Laws require verification of certain information about people claiming Benefits (e.g., age and family relationship to the worker) before either country can approve the claim. Article 4.4 provides that when a person files a claim for Benefits under the Agreement in one country, the Competent Institution of that country will verify the relevant information and inform the Liaison Institution of the other country of its findings. The Liaison Institutions will agree upon the specific types of information requiring verification.
This provision expedites the claims process by avoiding duplicate verification of the same information. A Competent Institution may still request additional evidence to support the finding of the other Competent Institution.

Chapter IV. Miscellaneous Provisions

Article 5
1) In accordance with measures to be decided pursuant to paragraph 2 of Article 2 of this Administrative Arrangement, the Liaison Institution of one Contracting State shall, upon request by the Liaison Institution of the other Contracting State, furnish available information relating to the claim of any specified individual for the purpose of administering the Agreement.[91]
2) For the purpose of facilitation of the implementation of the Agreement and this Administrative Arrangement, the Liaison Institutions may decide on measures for the electronic exchange of data.[92]

Article 6

The Liaison Institutions shall exchange statistics on the number of certificates issued under Article 3 of this Administrative Arrangement and on the payments made to beneficiaries under the Agreement. These statistics shall be furnished annually in a manner to be decided by the Liaison Institutions.[93]

Article 7
1) Where assistance is requested and provided under Article 10 of the Agreement, expenses other than regular personnel and operating costs shall be reimbursed to the Competent Institution providing the assistance, except as may be otherwise decided by the

---

[91] Article 5.1 provides that the Liaison Institution of one country will, upon request, furnish claims related information to the Liaison Institution of the other country in accordance with agreed upon procedures. Such procedures will be decided upon by the Liaison Institutions and will be consistent with the governing statutes of both countries.
[92] Under Article 5.2, the Liaison Institutions of both countries may choose to implement electronic data exchanges to facilitate administration of the Agreement and this Administrative Arrangement. Such exchanges must comply with the laws of each country governing the protection of privacy and confidentiality of Personal Data.
[93] Article 6 provides for an exchange of statistics concerning certificates issued pursuant to Article 3.1 of this Administrative Arrangement and payments made to beneficiaries under the Agreement.

Competent Authorities or Liaison Institutions of the Contracting States.[94]

2) Upon request, the Liaison Institution of either Contracting State shall furnish without cost to the Liaison Institution of the other Contracting State any medical information and documentation in its possession to assess the disability of the claimant or beneficiary.[95]

3) Medical examinations of persons who reside in the territory of one of the Contracting States, which are required under the Laws of the other Contracting State, shall be arranged by the Liaison Institution of the first Contracting State, upon the request and at the expense of the requesting Liaison Institution. The costs of medical examinations shall not be refunded if they are performed for the use of the Competent Institutions of both Contracting States.[96]

4) The Liaison Institution of one Contracting State shall reimburse amounts owed under paragraph 1 or 3 of this Article upon presentation of a statement of expenses by the Liaison Institution of the other Contracting State.[97]

---

[94] In accordance with Article 10 of the Agreement, the Competent Institutions of the two countries will provide each other with administrative assistance required to implement the Agreement. Under Article 7.1, the requesting Competent Institution will pay expenses the other Competent Institution incurs in responding to requests for administrative assistance that require it to go outside its own organization unless the two countries agree on a different arrangement. This includes hiring interpreters, conducting special field investigations, or arranging medical examinations. The Competent Institutions will not reimburse expenses for regular personnel and operating costs.

[95] When the Liaison Institution in one country requests medical information from the Liaison Institution in the other country, the other Liaison Institution will provide the requesting Liaison Institution with any pertinent medical records it has in its possession free of charge.

[96] Article 7.3 provides that where a medical examination is necessary to establish eligibility for or continuing entitlement to a country's Benefits that are payable under the Agreement, and the claimant or beneficiary is in the other country, the Liaison Institution of the other country, upon request, will arrange for the examination at the expense of the Liaison Institution requesting the examination.

[97] In order to receive reimbursement for the cost of administrative assistance, the Liaison Institution that provides the assistance must provide the requesting Liaison Institution with a statement of expenses.

Article 8

This Administrative Arrangement shall enter into force on the date of entry into force of the Agreement and remain in force as long as the Agreement is in force. [98]

DONE at Montevideo, this 10th day of January, 2017, in duplicate in the English and Spanish languages, both texts being equally authentic.[99]

For the Competent Authority of the United States of America:
Kelly Keiderling
For the Competent Authority of the Oriental Republic of Uruguay:
Ernesto Murro

---

[98] This Administrative Arrangement will enter into force on the same date as the Agreement and will remain in effect for the same period as the Agreement.

[99] The U.S. Ambassador to Uruguay, Kelly Keiderling, and the Uruguayan Minister of Labour and Social Affairs, Ernesto Murro, signed the Administrative Arrangement on January 10, 2017 in Montevideo.

Chapter 3

AGREEMENT ON SOCIAL SECURITY BETWEEN THE UNITED STATES AND THE REPUBLIC OF SLOVENIA[*]

Message from the President of the United States

To the Congress of the United States:

Pursuant to section 233(e)(1) of the Social Security Act, as amended by the Social Security Amendments of 1977 (Public Law 95–216, 42 U.S.C. 433(e)(1)), I transmit herewith a social security totalization agreement with Slovenia, titled "Agreement on Social Security between the United States of America and the Republic of Slovenia" and the accompanying legally binding administrative arrangement, titled "Administrative Arrangement between the United States of America and the Republic of Slovenia for the Implementation of the Agreement on Social Security between the United States of America and the Republic of

---

[*] This is an edited, reformatted and augmented version of 115th Congress, 2d Session, Publication No. House Document 115–125, dated MAY 17, 2018.

Slovenia" (collectively the "Agreements"). The Agreements were signed in Ljubljana, Slovenia, on January 17, 2017.

The Agreements are similar in objective and content to the social security totalization agreements already in force with other leading economic partners in Europe and elsewhere, including Australia, Canada, Chile, Japan, Norway, the Republic of Korea, and Switzerland. Such bilateral agreements provide for limited coordination between the United States and foreign social security systems to eliminate dual social security coverage and taxation and to help prevent the loss of benefit protection that can occur when workers divide their careers between two countries.

The Agreements contain all provisions mandated by section 233 of the Social Security Act and, pursuant to section 233(c)(4), other provisions which I deem appropriate to carry out the purposes of section 233.

I also transmit for the information of the Congress a report required by section 233(e)(1) of the Social Security Act on the estimated number of individuals who will be affected by the Agreements and the Agreements' estimated cost effect. Also included are a summary of the main provisions of the Agreements and an annotated version of the Agreements with descriptions of each article. The Department of State and the Social Security Administration concluded that these Agreements are in the national interest of the United States.

I commend to the Congress the Agreement on Social Security between the United States of America and the Republic of Slovenia and the Administrative Arrangement between the United States of America and the Republic of Slovenia for the Implementation of the Agreement on Social Security between the United States of America and the Republic of Slovenia.

Donald J. Trump
The White House,
May 17, 2018.

MAIN PROVISIONS OF THE UNITED STATES-SLOVENIA SOCIAL SECURITY AGREEMENT

Introduction

In general, section 233(c)(l) of the Social Security Act ("Act") requires that international agreements concluded pursuant to that section meet three requirements:

- They must eliminate dual coverage of the same work under the social security systems of the United States and the other country.
- They must allow for combining credits that the worker earns under the two systems for benefit eligibility purposes.
- When combined credits establish eligibility for U.S. Social Security benefits, the basis for the U.S. benefit payable must be the proportion of the worker's periods of coverage completed under title II of the Act.

The U.S.-Slovenia agreement includes these required provisions.

Elimination of Dual Coverage

The agreement establishes rules to eliminate dual coverage and taxation, the situation that now exists when a person from either the United States or Slovenia works in the other country. The agreement sets forth a general rule under which the social security system of the country where the employee performs the work will cover the employee, subject to the following exceptions:

- If an employer sends an employee from one of the agreement countries to work in the other country for a period not expected to exceed five years, the agreement provides that the employee will remain covered under the social security system of the country from which he or she was sent. Under a separate provision of the agreement, this same rule applies to a self-employed person who moves to work in the other country for a period not expected to exceed five years.

- Thus, a person whose U.S. employer temporarily transfers him or her to Slovenia will retain coverage under, and pay contributions to, the U.S. program exclusively. The agreement will relieve the employer and employee (or self-employed person) of the additional burden of paying social security contributions to the Slovenian program.
- The agreement also sets forth special coverage rules for employees of the governments of the two countries and for workers in international air and maritime transportation.

Totalization Benefit Provisions

The agreement will also help prevent situations where workers suffer a loss of benefit rights because they divide their careers between the United States and Slovenia.

Under the rules that apply to the United States, if a person has:

- credit for at least six quarters of coverage under the U.S. Social Security system; and
- not enough credits under the U.S. Social Security system to qualify for a retirement, survivors, or disability benefit,

The United States will totalize (i.e., combine) the worker's coverage credits from both countries for the purpose of determining eligibility for a U.S. retirement, survivors, or disability benefit. A person is eligible for a benefit if the worker meets the requirements for a benefit under the U.S. Social Security system based on the combined credits. The benefit amount payable to a person who qualifies based on totalized credits is proportional to the amount of coverage completed in the United States.

Under the rules that apply to Slovenia, if a person does not have enough total or recent coverage under the Slovene system to qualify for a retirement, survivors, or disability benefit, Slovenia will totalize the worker's coverage credits from both countries for the purpose of determining eligibility for a Slovene retirement, survivors, or disability benefit Where combined credits from both countries establish eligibility, Slovenia will compute a theoretical benefit amount as if the worker had completed his or her U.S. periods of coverage under Slovene law. To determine the benefit amoup.t actually payable, Slovenia will prorate the theoretical amount by multiplying it by the ratio of the periods of coverage credited under Slovene law to the total periods credited in both countries.

If a person qualifies for a benefit from the social security system of either country without the need to use credits the worker earned under the other country's social security system, a totalized benefit will not be paid by the country under whose laws the person qualifies; rather, a non-totalized benefit will be paid. However, entitlement to such benefit shall not preclude entitlement to a totalized benefit from the social security system of the other country, provided the person meets all the applicable requirements.

UNITED STATES-SLOVENIA
ADMINISTRATIVE ARRANGEMENT

Purpose

The administrative arrangement establishes a number of principles which will serve as the basis for developing operating procedures. In particular, it authorizes the designated liaison agencies to develop procedures and forms necessary to implement the principal agreement. The liaison agencies are:

- for the United States, the Social Security Administration (SSA); and
- for Slovenia, jointly the Pension and Disability Insurance Institute of Slovenia (PDII) and the Healthcare Insurance Institute of Slovenia (HII).

Elimination of Dual Coverage

The administrative arrangement sets forth rules for issuing the documentation necessary to exempt workers covered under one country's system from coverage under the other country's system. These rules provide that the Agency (as defined in the agreement) whose coverage laws will apply to a person working in the other country will, upon request, issue. A certificate of coverage. The certificate shall serve as proof of exemption from social security tax obligations under the other country's social security system.

Benefit Provisions

SSA and the Liaison Agency of Slovenia will exchange coverage records and other information required to process benefit claims filed under the agreement. The administrative arrangement sets forth procedures governing this exchange of claims-related information.

Principal Agreement: Agreement on Social Security between the United States of America and the Republic of Slovenia

The United States of America and The Republic of Slovenia (hereinafter individually known as "Contracting State" or collectively as

"Contracting States"), Being desirous of regulating the relationship between the two countries in the field of social security, have agreed as follows:

Part I. General Provisions

Article 1: Definitions[1]
1) For the purposes of the Agreement on Social Security between the United States of America and the Republic of Slovenia (hereinafter "Agreement"):
    a) "National" means,
        as regards the United States, a national of the United States as defined in Section 101, Immigration and Nationality Act, as amended, and
        as regards the Republic of Slovenia, a national of the Republic of Slovenia as defined in the Citizenship of the Republic of Slovenia Act, as amended;[2]
    b) "Laws" means the laws and regulations specified in Article 2 of this Agreement;[3]

---

[1] Article 1 defines key terms used in this Agreement.

[2] Under section 101(a)(22) of the Immigration and Nationality Act, "the term 'national of the United States' means (A) a citizen of the United States, or (B) a person who, though not a citizen of the United States, owes permanent allegiance to the United States." Those in category (B) include natives of American Samoa.
The Act on Citizenship of the Republic of Slovenia of 7 December 2006 specifies the categories of persons to whom the Republic of Slovenia ("Slovenia") accords citizenship. A Slovenian citizen is any person whom Slovenia accords citizenship.
This includes persons born to Slovenian parents, persons born in the territory of Slovenia whose parents are unknown or whose citizenship is unknown, persons who have become naturalized through specific application, and persons to whom an international agreement accords Slovenian citizenship.
Citizenship in Slovenia can be lost by means of release, renunciation, deprivation, or under the terms of an international agreement.

[3] The term "Laws," as used in this Agreement, refers to each country's social security laws and regulations as set forth in Article 2.

c) "Competent Authority" means,[4]
as regards the United States, the Commissioner of Social Security, and
as regards the Republic of Slovenia, the competent ministries with the powers conferred by the legislative acts defined in Article 2 of this Agreement;

d) "Agency" means,[5]
as regards the United States, the Social Security Administration, and
as regards the Republic of Slovenia, the institutions, funds and bodies, responsible for the implementation of the Laws defined in Article 2, Paragraph 1, subparagraph b of this Agreement;

e) "Period of Coverage" means a period of payment of contributions or a period of earnings from employment or self-employment, as defined or recognized as a period of coverage by the Laws under which such period has been completed, or any similar period in-so-far as it is recognized by such Laws as equivalent to a period of coverage; [6]

---

[4] "Competent Authority," wherever it appears in this Agreement, refers to the government official in each country with ultimate responsibility for administering the social security program and the provisions of this Agreement.

[5] "Agency," as used in this Agreement, refers to the administrative body in each country responsible for taking and processing claims and making coverage determinations under each country's social security Laws.
The Social Security Administration (SSA) is the Agency for the United States. However, the U.S. Internal Revenue Service (IRS) retains its responsibility for determining Social Security tax liability based on SSA coverage determinations under this Agreement.
For Slovenia, the Agency is the Institute for Pension and Invalidity Insurance of Slovenia (IPII). Other compulsory programs of social insurance in Slovenia that are not included in the OASDI program (health insurance, work injury, unemployment, etc.) from which U.S. workers will be exempt by virtue of Part II of this Agreement are administered by other Slovenian Agencies which, while not responsible for the provision of Benefits under this Agreement, still maintain administrative control over those programs (See Article 2.1 (b)(ii)).

[6] "Period of Coverage" means any period credited under the social security Laws of either country for purposes of determining Benefit eligibility, including periods of covered employment and self-employment.

Agreement on Social Security between the United States ... 149

    f) "**Benefit**" means any benefit provided for in the Laws specified in Article 2 of this Agreement;[7]

    g) "**Personal Data**" means any information relating to a specific (identified or identifiable) person, as well as any information that can be used to distinguish or trace an individual's identity. This includes, but is not limited to, the following: any individual identifier; citizenship, nationality, statelessness, or refugee status; benefits, eligibility, or other claims information; contact information; medical information or lay information used in a medical determination; information about marital, familial, or personal relationships; and information pertaining to work, financial, or economic status; and[8]

    h) "**Liaison Agencies**" means institutions authorized to route inquiries and correspondence for effective implementation of this Agreement.[9]

2. Any term not defined in this Article shall have the meaning assigned to it in the applicable Laws.[10]

Article 2: Material Scope

    1) For the purposes of this Agreement, the applicable Laws are: [11]

---

[7] "Benefit" refers to old-age, survivors, and disability Benefits provided under the social security Laws of either country. With respect to the United States, the term also includes the lump-sum death payment under section 202(i) of the Social Security Act ("Act"). It also excludes special age-72 payments provided for certain uninsured persons under section 228 of the Act.

[8] "Personal data" refers to personally identifiable information. Since there is no definition of "personal data" in the Act, this term incorporates and expands upon essential elements of the definition of "information" applying to SSA at 20 CFR 401.25.

[9] Article 2 of the Administrative Arrangement designates the agencies in each country that will coordinate implementation and administration of this Agreement's coverage and Benefit provisions. SSA is the designated Liaison Agency for the United States. The counterpart Liaison Agencies for Slovenia are the IPII and the Health Insurance Institute of Slovenia (HII).

[10] If this Agreement does not define a term, that term has the same meaning as it does under each country's national laws.

[11] Article 2.1 specifies the Laws to which this Agreement applies.

a) as regards the United States, the laws governing the Federal old-age, survivors, and disability insurance program:
   i. Title II of the Social Security Act and regulations pertaining thereto, except sections 226, 226A, and 228 of that title, and regulations pertaining to those sections, and[12]
   ii. Chapters 2 and 21 of the Internal Revenue Code of 1986 and regulations pertaining to those chapters; and[13]
b) as regards the Republic of Slovenia:
   i. the laws governing pension and disability insurance, except the provisions on residual working capacity, and[14]
   ii. with regard to Part II of this Agreement only, the laws of the Republic of Slovenia governing the compulsory participation in social insurance system. [15]

2) Unless otherwise provided in this Agreement, the Laws referred to in paragraph 1 of this Article shall not include treaties or other international agreements or supranational legislation on Social Security concluded between one Contracting State and a third State, or laws or regulations promulgated for their specific implementation.[16]

---

[12] For the United States, this Agreement applies to title II of the Act. It also applies to the corresponding tax laws (the Federal Insurance Contributions Act-FICA and the Self-Employment Contributions Act-SECA) and any regulations pertaining to those laws. This Agreement does not apply to Medicare provisions (sections 226 and 226A of the Act). It also does not apply to provisions for special payments to uninsured individuals age 72 or over under section 228 of the Act. Persons to whom this Agreement applies who qualify for Medicare hospital insurance or age-72 payments without application of this Agreement may still receive such benefits.

[13] A worker subject only to U.S. Laws under the coverage provisions of this Agreement and his or her employer will be exempt from making contributions for Slovenian OASDI, maternity, sickness, work injury, unemployment insurance, and health insurance programs.

[14] For Slovenia, this Agreement applies to the Laws governing the old-age, survivors, and disability insurance (OASDI) Benefits programs of the social security system.

[15] A worker subject only to U.S. Laws under the coverage provisions of this Agreement and his or her employer will be exempt from making contributions for Slovenian OASDI, maternity, sickness, work injury, unemployment insurance, and health insurance programs.

[16] Except as this Agreement itself provides, the Laws to which the Agreement applies do not include treaties and other international agreements. This includes either country's bilateral social security agreements with third countries or multilateral agreements. This provision ensures that if a person has Periods of Coverage in the United States and Slovenia and periods of coverage in a third country with which either country has a social security

3) No provision in this Agreement shall affect the obligation of either Contracting State's social security agreements or any other international agreements by which either Contracting State is bound.[17]

4) Except as provided in the following sentence, this Agreement shall also apply to laws and regulations that amend or supplement the Laws specified in paragraph 1 of this Article. This Agreement shall apply to future laws and regulations of a Contracting State which create new categories of beneficiaries or new Benefits under the Laws of that Contracting State unless the Competent Authority of that Contracting State notifies the Competent Authority of the other Contracting State in writing within three (3) months of the date of the official publication of the new laws or regulations that no such extension of this Agreement is intended.[18]

Article 3: Persons Covered

This Agreement shall apply[19]:

a) to any person who is or has been subject to the Laws of either Contracting State, and

---

agreement, SSA cannot combine periods from all three countries to meet U.S. Benefit eligibility requirements.

[17] This paragraph provides that none of the provisions of this Agreement affect Slovenia's commitments under any bilateral or multilateral agreements or other arrangements. These include, but are not limited to, its obligations under European Union (EU) rules, its agreements as a member of the European Economic Area (EEA), and its bilateral agreements with other countries.

[18] Article 2.4 provides that this Agreement will automatically apply to any future U.S. or Slovenian legislation that amends or supplements the Laws set forth in paragraph 1. This includes legislation that creates new categories of beneficiaries or new Benefits. The country enacting the legislation may exclude it from the scope of this Agreement by giving written notice to the other country within 3 months of the legislation's official publication.

[19] Article 3 specifies the persons to whom this Agreement applies. These include persons currently or previously covered under U.S. or Slovenian Laws. This Agreement also applies to the dependents and survivors of such persons when the Laws of one or both countries confer rights to dependents or survivors because of their relationship to such persons.

b) to the dependents and survivors of a person described in subparagraph (a) of this Article within the meaning of the applicable Laws of either Contracting State.

Article 4: Equality of Treatment
1) Unless otherwise provided in this Agreement, persons described in Article 3 of this Agreement who reside in the territory of one Contracting State shall receive equal treatment with Nationals of the second Contracting State in the application of the Laws of the second Contracting State. [20]
2) Unless otherwise provided in this Agreement, any provision of the Laws of a Contracting State which restricts entitlement to or payment of Benefits solely because a person resides outside or is absent from the territory of that Contracting State shall not be applicable to a person who resides in the territory of the other Contracting State.[21]

---

[20] Article 4.1 provides that persons to whom this Agreement applies who reside in the United States or Slovenia will receive the same treatment as that country gives its own Nationals. Article 6.7 of this Agreement limits this provision to ensure that any equal treatment accorded in this paragraph does not contravene existing U.S. law.
The intent of this provision is to eliminate discrimination based on a person's nationality with respect to Benefits. It would not affect U.S. restrictions on Benefit eligibility or payment because a person is not lawfully present in that country or did not have permission to work in that country. The provision also does not affect the coverage provisions of either country's Laws, since Part II of the Agreement deals with social security coverage.

[21] Article 4.2 provides that where the Laws of either country require residence in that country in order to qualify for or receive social security Benefits, a person may also qualify for and receive those Benefits while residing in the other country. By virtue of an exchange of diplomatic notes in 1959 between the United States and the former Socialist Federal Republic of Yugoslavia and SSA's published finding about Slovenia's social security system (see 79 Fed. Reg. 42,867), the United States has long paid benefits to Slovenian (formerly Yugoslav) citizens who do not satisfy U.S. residency requirements for Benefit payment contained in section 202(t)(1) of the Act. However, the nonpayment exception is subject to other U.S. payment restrictions based on residency requirements for dependents and survivors; e.g., section 202(t)(11) of the Act. Both countries intend that under this Agreement, Nationals of either country may qualify for or receive Benefits while residing in the other country. Accordingly, under section 233(c)(2) of the Act, this Agreement will permit the United States to pay dependents and survivors currently subject to such residency requirements as well as certain persons who are third country nationals residing in either country.

Part II. Provisions Concerning Applicable Laws[22]

Article 5: Coverage Provisions
1) Except as otherwise provided in this Article, a person employed or self-employed within the territory of one of the Contracting States, with respect to that employment or self-employment, shall be subject to the Laws of only that Contracting State.[23]
2) Where a person who is normally employed in the territory of one Contracting State by an employer in that territory is sent by that employer to the territory of the other Contracting State for a temporary period that is not expected to exceed five (5) years, the person shall be subject to the Laws of only the first Contracting State as if the person were employed in the territory of the first Contracting State.[24]
3) For purposes of applying paragraph 2 of this Article in the case of an employee who is sent from the territory of the United States by an employer in that territory to the territory of the Republic of Slovenia, that employer and an affiliated company of the employer (as defined under the laws of the United States) shall be considered

---

[22] Part II eliminates dual social security coverage, which occurs when a worker must pay social security taxes to both countries for the same earnings. This Agreement complies with the existing coverage provisions under the Laws of both countries except when necessary to prevent payment of social security taxes to both countries for the same earnings. The provisions in this Part retain the worker's social security coverage and taxation in the country to whose economy he or she has the more direct connection, while exempting the worker from coverage and taxation under the other country's system.

[23] Article 5.1 establishes a basic territoriality rule, stating that ordinarily, only the country in which a person is working will compulsorily cover the person's work in that country. Work that both countries would otherwise cover will remain covered exclusively under the system of the country where the person is working. Such work activity will be exempt from coverage under the other country's system.

[24] Under Article 5.2, an employee who normally works for an employer located in the United States or in Slovenia who temporarily transfers to work in the other country for the same employer will continue to pay social security taxes to the system of the country from which the employee transferred. This rule will apply only if the employer expects the period of transfer to be 5 years or less.
In determining the length of a transfer for workers whose employer sent them from one country to the other before this Agreement entered into force, both countries will ignore any period of work before this Agreement's entry into force. (See Article 20.3).

one and the same, provided that the employment would have been covered under United States Laws absent this Agreement.[25]

4) Paragraphs 2 and 3 of this Article shall apply where a person who has been sent by his or her employer from the territory of a Contracting State to the territory of a third State, and who is compulsorily covered under the Laws of that Contracting State while employed in the territory of the third State, is subsequently sent by that employer from the territory of the third State to the territory of the other Contracting State.[26]

5) A person who is normally self-employed in the territory of one Contracting State, and who temporarily transfers his or her self-employment activity to the territory of the other Contracting State shall be subject to the Laws of only the first Contracting State, provided that the period of self-employment activity in the territory of the other Contracting State is not expected to exceed five (5) years.[27]

   a) A person who is employed as an officer or member of a crew on a vessel which flies the flag of one Contracting State and who would be covered under the Laws of both Contracting States shall be subject to the Laws of only the Contracting

---

[25] Article 5.3 broadens the scope of Article 5.2 to include certain workers whose employers in the United States send them to work for a subsidiary or other affiliate of that employer in Slovenia. U.S. law allows American companies to extend U.S. Social Security coverage to U.S. citizens and resident aliens employed by an affiliated company in another country. To do this, the parent company in the United States must enter into an agreement with the IRS to pay Social Security contributions on behalf of all U.S. citizens and residents the foreign affiliate employs. Under Article 5.2, U.S. citizens or resident aliens an American employer sends to work for a Slovenian affiliate for 5 years or less will continue to have coverage in the United States and be exempt from Slovenian coverage and contributions, if an IRS agreement covers the affiliate.

[26] Under Article 5.4, the provisions of Articles 5.2 and 5.3 will apply even if an employee did not transfer directly from one country to the other, but first transferred to work in a third country.

[27] Article 5.5 provides that a person who is self-employed in one country who transfers his or her trade or business to the other country for a period of 5 years or less will remain covered only by the country from which he or she moved. This rule will apply only if the self-employed person expects the period of transfer to last 5 years or less.

In determining the duration of such a transfer for a person who moves his or her business to the other country before this Agreement enters into force, Article 20.3 provides that both countries will ignore any period of self-employment before the Agreement's entry into force.

State whose flag the vessel flies. For purposes of the preceding sentence, a vessel which flies the flag of the United States is one defined as an American vessel under the Laws of the United States.[28]

b) Traveling employees of air transportation companies who perform work in the territories of both Contracting States and who would otherwise be covered under the Laws of both Contracting States shall, with respect to that work, be subject to the Laws of only the Contracting State in the territory of which the company has its headquarters. However, if such employees reside in the territory of the other Contracting State, they shall be subject to the Laws of only that Contracting State.[29]

6) (a) This Agreement shall not affect the provisions of the Vienna Convention on Diplomatic Relations of April 18, 1961, or of the Vienna Convention on Consular Relations of April 24, 1963.[30]

---

[28] Article 5.6(a) states that an employee on a U.S. or Slovenian ship, who would otherwise have coverage in both countries, will have coverage only in the country whose flag the ship flies. U.S. law considers a ship to fly the flag of the United States if the Act defines it as an American vessel. Section 210(c) of the Act defines an American vessel as one that is, "documented or numbered under the laws of the United States; and includes any vessel which is neither documented or numbered under the laws of the United States nor documented under the laws of any foreign country, if its crew is employed solely by one or more citizens or residents of the United States or corporations organized under the laws of the United States or of any State."

[29] Under Article 5.6(b), a member of the flight crew of an aircraft operating between the United States and Slovenia who would otherwise have coverage in both countries will have coverage only in the country in which the company employing the person has its headquarters. However, if the employee resides in the other country, he or she will only have coverage in that country.

[30] Article 5.7(a) specifies that the coverage provisions of this Agreement will not affect the relevant provisions of the Vienna Conventions on Diplomatic and Consular Relations. The Vienna Conventions, to which both the United States and Slovenia are parties, address the application of social security provisions in force in the receiving state to diplomatic agents, members of the administrative and technical staffs, member of consular posts and family members of such staff who form part of their households, the service staffs of the missions, and private servants whom the members of such missions employ.
The Vienna Conventions usually exempt such persons from social security coverage and contributions in the host country with respect to services rendered for the sending state, with certain limited exceptions. Persons who do not enjoy an exemption under the Conventions would be subject to the Laws of the host country and the coverage provisions of this Agreement, including Article 5.7 (b), if applicable.

(b) Nationals of one of the Contracting States who are employed by the Government of that Contracting State in the territory of the other Contracting State but who are not exempt from the Laws of the other Contracting State by virtue of the Vienna Conventions mentioned in subparagraph (a) of this paragraph shall be subject to the Laws of only the first Contracting State. For the purpose of this paragraph, employment by the United States Government includes employment by an instrumentality thereof.[31]

7) The Competent Authorities of the two Contracting States may agree to grant an exception to the provisions of this Article with respect to particular persons or categories of persons, provided that any affected person shall be subject to the Laws of one of the Contracting States.[32]

Part III. Provisions on Benefits[33]

Article 6: United States Benefits[34]

1) Where a person has completed at least six (6) quarters of coverage under United States Laws, but does not have sufficient Periods of Coverage to satisfy the requirements for entitlement to Benefits

---

[31] Under Article 5.7(b), if a U.S. or Slovenian National works for his or her country's Government in the other country, but the Vienna Conventions do not provide an exemption to this person, the person will be subject only to his or her country's Laws. This provision applies to U.S. Government and Slovenian Government employees, as well as to persons working for a U.S. Government instrumentality.

[32] Under Article 5.8, either country may grant an exception to the coverage rules of this Agreement if the other country agrees and the person involved retains coverage in one of the countries. Either country may grant such an exception to an individual worker or to all workers under similar circumstances, e.g., in the same profession or working for the same employer. This provision allows the Competent Authorities to resolve anomalous coverage situations that are unfavorable to workers or to eliminate dual coverage in unforeseen circumstances.

[33] Part III establishes the basic rules for determining social security Benefit entitlement when an individual has coverage in both countries. It sets out the rules for determining Benefit amounts when entitlement is possible only with combined work credits. Article 6 deals with the U.S. system, and Article 7 contains rules applicable to the Slovenian system.

[34] Article 6 contains rules for using combined coverage to determine U.S. Benefit eligibility and amounts.

under United States Laws, the Agency of the United States shall take into account, for the purpose of establishing entitlement to Benefits under this Article, Periods of Coverage which are credited under Republic of Slovenia Laws and which do not coincide with Periods of Coverage already credited under United States Laws.[35]

2) In determining eligibility for Benefits under paragraph 1 of this Article, the Agency of the United States shall credit one (1) quarter of coverage for every ninety (90) days of coverage certified by the Agency of the Republic of Slovenia. The total number of quarters of coverage to be credited for a year shall not exceed four (4).[36]

3) Where it is not possible to determine the calendar quarter during which a specific Period of Coverage was completed under the Laws of the United States, the United States Agency will presume that the Period of Coverage does not coincide with a Period of Coverage completed in the Republic of Slovenia.[37]

4) The Agency of the United States shall not take into account Periods of Coverage that occurred prior to the earliest date for which Periods of Coverage may be credited under its Laws, nor

---

[35] Under Article 6.1, if a person has at least six U.S. quarters of coverage, but not enough quarters to qualify for U.S. Benefits, SSA will take into account any Periods of Coverage that Slovenian Laws credit, if these periods do not coincide with quarters of coverage that the United States already credited.

[36] Article 6.2 establishes how SSA will convert Periods of Coverage under the Slovenian system into equivalent periods under the U.S. system. The U.S. system measures Periods of Coverage in terms of calendar quarters while the Slovenian system measures Periods of Coverage in days, months, and years.

Beginning in 1978, SSA bases quarters of coverage on the amount of a person's annual earnings (e.g., for 2017, $1,300 in earnings equals one quarter of coverage). Under Article 6.2, SSA will credit one quarter of coverage in a calendar year for every 90 days of coverage that the Slovenian Agency certifies for that year. (Article 7.5 provides a corresponding rule for converting U.S. quarters of coverage into Slovenian Periods of Coverage when determining Slovenian Benefit eligibility.)

SSA will not credit more than 4 quarters of coverage for any calendar year. SSA will also not credit months of coverage under Slovenian Laws that fall within a calendar quarter that SSA already credited as a U.S. quarter of coverage.

[37] Since 1978, SSA has credited quarters of coverage based on a worker's total earnings in a given calendar year. It is not generally possible to determine the period in any given calendar year during which a person worked. Accordingly, where necessary, SSA credits Periods of Coverage within such calendar year in a manner to entitle the worker and his or her dependents or survivors to Benefits (see 20 C.F.R. § 404.1908 (b)(2)).

will the Agency of the United States take into account any Periods of Coverage that are not based on paid contributions. [38]

5) Where entitlement to a Benefit under United States Laws is established according to the provisions of paragraph 1 of this Article, the Agency of the United States shall compute a pro rata Primary Insurance Amount in accordance with United States Laws based on

   a) the person's average earnings credited exclusively under United States Laws and

   b) the ratio of the duration of the person's Periods of Coverage completed under United States Laws to the duration of a coverage lifetime as determined in accordance with United States Laws.

Benefits payable under United States Laws shall be based on the pro rata Primary Insurance Amount. [39]

6) Entitlement to a Benefit from the United States that results from paragraph 1 of this Article shall terminate with the acquisition of sufficient Periods of Coverage under United States Laws to

---

[38] For purposes of entitlement to Benefits under this Agreement, SSA will not consider periods of Slovenian coverage credited prior to 1937, the earliest date for which U.S. law permits crediting Periods of Coverage. SSA also will not consider Slovenian Periods of Coverage that are not based on a worker's paid contributions to the Slovenian system.

[39] Article 6.5 describes the method of computing U.S. Benefit amounts when SSA establishes entitlement by totalizing (i.e., combining) U.S. and Slovenian coverage. Persons whose U.S. coverage alone qualifies them for U.S. Benefits will not receive U.S. totalization Benefits.
Under Article 6.5, the amount of the worker's Benefit depends on both the level of his or her earnings and the duration of his or her U.S. Social Security coverage. SSA regulations (20 CFR 404.1918) describe this computation procedure in detail.
The first step in the procedure is to compute a theoretical Primary Insurance Amount (PIA) as though the worker had spent a full career under U.S. Social Security at the same level of earnings as during his or her actual periods of U.S. covered work. SSA then prorates the theoretical PIA to reflect the proportion of a coverage lifetime completed under the U.S. program. The regulations define a coverage lifetime as the number of years used in determining a worker's average earnings under the regular U.S. national computation method.

Agreement on Social Security between the United States ... 159

establish entitlement to an equal or higher Benefit without the need to invoke the provision of paragraph 1 of this Article. [40]

7) Article 4 of this Agreement shall be applied by the United States in a manner consistent with section 233(c)(4) of the United States Social Security Act.[41]

Article 7: Republic of Slovenia Benefits

1) Where the requirements for entitlement to Benefits under Republic of Slovenia Laws are satisfied without the Periods of Coverage under United States Laws, the Republic of Slovenia Agency shall provide Benefits for the Periods of Coverage exclusively completed under Republic of Slovenia Laws. [42]

---

[40] Article 6.6 provides that if a worker entitled to a U.S. totalization Benefit acquires additional U.S. coverage that enables the worker to qualify for an equal or higher Benefit based only on his or her U.S. coverage, SSA will pay the regular national law Benefit rather than the totalization Benefit.

[41] Section 233(c)(1) and (2) of the Act specifies certain benefit and coverage provisions which either must be or may be included in U.S. international Social Security agreements. In addition, section 233(c)(4) permits agreements to contain other unspecified provisions which are not inconsistent with the provisions of title II of the Act. Article 6.7 is intended to make clear that where the only authority for the equality of treatment provisions in Article 4 of this Agreement is section 233(c)(4) of the Act, these provisions will be applied by the United States only to the extent that they do not conflict with other provisions of title II of the Act.

[42] Slovenia pays social security benefits to workers who meet the applicable eligibility standards, including minimum length of coverage and other requirements. Under Article 7, Slovenia will add a person's U.S. coverage to his or her Slovenian coverage, if necessary, to meet eligibility rules. If the person meets the requirements based on combined U.S. and Slovenian coverage, Slovenia will pay a partial benefit proportional to the amount of coverage credited under the Slovenian system.

SLOVENIAN SOCIAL SECURITY BENEFITS

GENERAL

The Slovenian social security system consists of a mandatory defined benefit pension financed on a pay-as-you-go basis, supplemented by a voluntary occupational pension system and a voluntary tax deductible savings scheme for employers and their employees. This Article applies to the defined benefit system, which is a contributory program that covers almost all residents of Slovenia.

Slovenia pays Benefits in amounts that it bases primarily on a percentage of a worker's average earnings, which varies based on the total number of years of contributions a worker has made into the Slovenian system and his or her gender. The voluntary pension system exists to supplement the basic Benefit and is not subject to this Agreement.

OLD-AGE BENEFITS

Effective with 2013 reforms, the retirement age in Slovenia is age 65 for males and females with at least 15 years of contributions to the Slovenian system. Early retirement is possible for workers who have worked for at least 40 years under the Slovenian system and have attained age 60. Prior to this reform, the retirement age could, under certain circumstances, be as low as 58, and females could retire several years earlier than males.

The Slovenian system requires a minimum of 15 years of coverage for entitlement to an old-age Benefit, but provides incentives in the form of a higher Benefit for workers making additional contributions to the system. In addition, a worker who meets the criteria for an early retirement Benefit is eligible for credits for deferring receipt of his or her Benefit past age 60.

The Slovenian old-age Benefit is calculated as 26% for males (29% for females) of the worker's most advantageous 24 year period of lifetime earnings. If a worker has fewer than 24 years of earnings, Slovenia will base the Benefit on his or her total career earnings. For each year of contribution over 15, Slovenia adds 1.25% to the percentage without limit. Additionally, workers who have attained age 60 and have at least 40 years of contributions are eligible for a Benefit increase for deferring receipt of the Benefit past age 60.

The statutory minimum pension amount since January 1, 2015 has been €199.99 (approximately $215) per month. While there is no statutory maximum pension amount, a worker's average earnings for purposes of calculating a Benefit cannot exceed €3,076.76 (approximately $3,300) per month.

DISABILITY BENEFITS

The Slovenian system pays Benefits to three categories of disability beneficiaries. Category I disabled workers are completely incapable of work. Category II disabled workers have lost at least 50% of their work capacity. Category III disabled workers can work at least 4 hours per day, but not without prior rehabilitation.

In order to qualify, workers age 30 or older must have worked for 1/3 of the period between attainment of age 20 and the date of disability onset. Workers age 21 – 29 must have worked at least 1/4 of the same period, and workers younger than 21 must have worked at least 3 months. In addition, Category II disabled workers must either be older than 55 or unable to be rehabilitated.

The amount of a disability Benefit depends on the worker's most advantageous 24 year period of lifetime earnings, the age at which he or she became disabled, and his or her gender. If a worker has fewer than 24 years of earnings, Slovenia will base the Benefit on his or her total career earnings. Workers who are disabled at an earlier age receive a higher percentage of the earnings they accrued prior to the disability onset, with a minimum of 36% for males and 39% for females. Category III disabled workers only receive a partial Benefit based on a number of different factors, including their ability to be rehabilitated.

The statutory minimum pension amount since January 1, 2015 has been €199.99 (approximately $215) per month. While there is no statutory maximum pension amount, a worker's average earnings for purposes of calculating a Benefit cannot exceed €3,076.76 (approximately $3,300) per month. The statutory minimum pension does not apply to Category III disabled workers.

SURVIVORS' BENEFITS

Survivors' Benefits are payable to the worker's widow(er)s, divorced spouses, surviving partners/cohabitants, children, stepchildren, adopted children, grandchildren, parents, adoptive parents, and grandparents.

Agreement on Social Security between the United States ... 161

2) Where the requirements for entitlements to Benefits under Republic of Slovenia Laws are not satisfied on the basis of Periods of Coverage completed under Republic of Slovenia Laws alone, the Republic of Slovenia Agency shall take into account, for the purpose of establishing entitlements to Benefits[43], Periods of Coverage which are credited under United States Laws and do not coincide with Periods of Coverage credited under Republic of Slovenia Laws.[44]

In order for survivors to be eligible to receive a Benefit, the worker must have been either in receipt of or eligible for an old-age or disability **Benefit.** In cases where a worker's death was related to an injury that he or she sustained at work, this requirement is waived.

Surviving spouses must be at least 53 at the time of the worker's death (receipt of the Benefit is deferred until age 58), disabled, caring for a child of the worker, or give birth to a child of the worker within 300 days of the worker's death. Surviving partners/cohabitants must additionally have either cohabitated for the 3 years prior to the worker's death or have cohabitated for at least the past year in case they had a child. For divorced spouses, the spouse must have been entitled to a maintenance right (alimony) prior to the worker's death. Any spouse, partner, or cohabitant is ineligible to receive a Benefit if he or she remarries or enters into a registered cohabitation prior to attaining age 58.

Benefits rise according to the Swiss Indexation method. This method uses a composite of changes in the consumer price index and changes in national wages to determine cost of living adjustments. Changes in the national wage level account for 60% of the cost of living adjustment (COLA), while changes in the consumer price index account for 40% of the COLA.

Children of the worker can receive a Benefit until age 15 under any circumstances, age 18 if registered at an employment office, age 26 if attending a secondary or tertiary level educational institution, or without age limit if disabled. Stepchildren, grandchildren, and adopted children must have additionally been in the worker's care at the time of his or her death. Parents, adoptive parents, **and** grandparents must have likewise been in the worker's care at the time of his or her death.

The amount of a survivors' **Benefit** varies depending on the number of other entitled beneficiaries. If only one survivor is eligible, then he or she receives 70% of the Benefit to which the worker would have been entitled. Two survivors will split 80% of the worker's Benefit, while three survivors will split 90%. Four or more survivors will all split 100% of the worker's Benefit amount.

COST-OF-LIVING ADJUSTMENTS

---

[43] Article 7.1 makes clear that a Slovenian Benefit based only on Slovenian Periods of Coverage will be payable unless a person is eligible only if the IPII credits both U.S. and Slovenian Periods of Coverage.

[44] Article 7.2 provides that if a person does not have enough Slovenian Periods of Coverage to qualify for Slovenian Benefits, the Slovenian Agency will add U.S. quarters of coverage to Slovenian Periods of Coverage in determining whether a person meets the minimum requirements for Benefits under Slovenian Laws. The Slovenian Agency will not consider

3) Where entitlement requirements under paragraph 2 of this Article are not satisfied, the Republic of Slovenia Agency shall also take into account the periods completed under the Laws of third countries with which the Republic of Slovenia has concluded international Social Security Agreements with provisions on the totalization of periods. [45]

4) When entitlement to Benefits is established through procedures referred to in paragraphs 2 and 3 of this Article, the Republic of Slovenia Agency shall calculate the Benefit amount as follows[46]:

   a) First, a theoretical amount of the Benefit which would be paid if all the totalized Periods of Coverage were completed under Republic of Slovenia Laws, is calculated.

   b) The theoretical amount is then used for the calculation of the actual amount of the Benefit to be paid in the proportional relation to the Period of Coverage completed under Republic of Slovenia Laws and other Periods of Coverage used for the purposes of totalization.

   c) The calculation of the theoretical amount of the Benefit referred to in subparagraph (a) of this paragraph for the purposes of the determination of the Benefit shall only take into account Periods of Coverage completed under the Republic of Slovenia Laws.

---

any U.S. Periods of Coverage that coincide with a Period of Coverage already credited under Slovenian Laws.

[45] Article 7.3 expands upon Article 7.2, stating that if a person does not have enough combined U.S. and Slovenian Periods of Coverage to qualify for Slovenian Benefits, the Slovenian Agency will also consider third country periods that do not coincide with Slovenian Periods of Coverage for purposes of entitlement to a Benefit.

[46] Article 7.4 describes the method for Slovenian Benefit computations under this Agreement. The Slovenian Agency will perform a three step Benefit calculation. Initially, it will combine Periods of Coverage in Slovenia and in the United States. If the combined coverage meets the length of coverage requirements under Slovenian Laws, the Slovenian Agency will then compute a theoretical Benefit amount using only Periods of Coverage acquired under Slovenian Laws. Finally, it will determine a pro rata Benefit amount by multiplying the theoretical amount by the ratio of the Periods of Coverage completed under Slovenian Laws to the total Periods of Coverage completed in both (or, as needed, multiple) countries.

5) When establishing the entitlement to Benefits referred to in paragraphs 2 and 3 of this Article, the Republic of Slovenia Agency shall equal each quarter reported by the United States Agency to a Period of Coverage of three (3) months.[47]
6) Where the total Periods of Coverage completed under Republic of Slovenia Laws amount to less than twelve (12) months, the Benefit shall not be granted. This provision does not apply if – under Republic of Slovenia Laws – the entitlement to Benefit exists solely on the basis of such a short Period of Coverage.[48]
7) Assistance and Attendance Allowance, Disability Allowance, Residual Working Capacity Benefit or any other noncontributory benefit which is not exportable under Republic of Slovenia Laws, shall be paid as long as the beneficiary resides in the territory of the Republic of Slovenia. [49]

Part IV. Miscellaneous Provisions

---

[47] In combining Periods of Coverage to determine Benefit eligibility, the Slovenian Agency will credit 3 months of coverage for each quarter of coverage SSA certifies. Article 6.2 provides a corresponding rule for converting Slovenian Periods of Coverage into U.S. quarters of coverage when determining U.S. Benefit eligibility.

[48] Under Article 7.6, the Slovenian system will not take U.S. Periods of Coverage into account under this Agreement if the worker has fewer than 12 months of Slovenian coverage and cannot establish entitlement to Slovenian Benefits based on Slovenian coverage alone (in certain circumstances, it is possible to qualify for Slovenian Benefits with less than one year of coverage).

Like the similar six quarters of coverage required for totalization by the United States under Article 6.1, this provision removes the considerable administrative burden of processing claims for very small Benefits based on minimal Periods of Coverage.

[49] Slovenia provides special classes of non-contributory, social assistance benefits paid from general tax revenues that are not exportable outside the territory of Slovenia. Article 7.7 stipulates that the Slovenian Agency will pay such social assistance benefits under this Agreement only to residents of Slovenia.

Article 8: Administrative Arrangements[50]

The Contracting States shall:
a) make all necessary administrative arrangements for the implementation of this Agreement and designate Liaison Agencies;
b) communicate to each other information concerning the measures taken for the application of this Agreement; and
c) communicate to each other, as soon as possible, information concerning all changes in their respective Laws which may affect the application of this Agreement.

Article 9: Mutual Assistance[51]

The Competent Authorities and the Agencies of the Contracting States, within the scope of their respective authorities, shall assist each other in implementing this Agreement. This assistance shall be free of charge, subject to exceptions to be agreed upon in an administrative arrangement.

Article 10: Confidentiality of Exchanged Personal Data

1) Unless otherwise required by the national statutes of a Contracting State, Personal Data transmitted in accordance with this Agreement to one Contracting State by the other Contracting State shall be used exclusively for purposes of administering this Agreement and the Laws referred to in Article 2 of this Agreement. The receiving Contracting State's national statutes for

---

[50] Article 8 outlines various duties of the Competent Authorities under this Agreement. Paragraph (a) authorizes and requires the Competent Authorities to conclude an Administrative Arrangement and designate Liaison Agencies to facilitate the implementation of this Agreement. Paragraph (b) requires them to notify each other of steps they take unilaterally to implement this Agreement. Paragraph (c) obligates the Competent Authorities to notify each other of any changes in their social security Laws that may affect the application of this Agreement.

[51] Article 9 authorizes the two countries to furnish each other non-reimbursable assistance in administering this Agreement. Such assistance may include taking Benefit applications and the gathering and exchange, including the electronic exchange, of information relevant to claims filed and Benefits paid under this Agreement. Although Article 9 establishes a general principle that mutual administrative assistance will be free of charge, the provision authorizes the two sides to agree to exceptions, such as the exception for medical examinations in Article 7.3 of the Administrative Arrangement.

the protection of privacy and confidentiality of Personal Data, and the provisions of this Agreement generally, shall govern such use.[52]

2) The Competent Authorities of the Contracting States shall inform each other about all amendments to their national statutes regarding the protection of privacy and confidentiality of Personal Data that affect the transmission of Personal Data.[53]

3) The Competent Authority or Agency requesting or transmitting Personal Data pursuant to this Agreement, upon request, must disclose to a person the following[54]:
   a) the content of his or her Personal Data,
   b) the Agency receiving his or her Personal Data,
   c) the duration of use of his or her Personal Data, and
   d) the purpose and legal grounds for which his or her Personal Data were used or requested.

4) The Competent Authority or Agency transmitting Personal Data pursuant to this Agreement shall, subject to the information available to the transmitting Contracting State, take all reasonable steps to ensure that transmitted Personal Data are accurate, up to date and limited to data required to fulfill the receiving Competent

---

[52] Both the United States and Slovenia recognize the great importance of ensuring the integrity of Personal Data, as well as a person's rights pertaining thereto. Accordingly, both countries have statutes and regulations that govern disclosure and provide strict safeguards for maintaining the confidentiality of Personal Data in the possession of their respective governments.
In the United States, these statutes include the Freedom of Information Act, the Privacy Act, section 6103 of the Internal Revenue Code, and pertinent provisions of the Act and other related statutes. In Slovenia, the applicable laws include the Personal Data Protection Act No. 86/2004 and EU Directive 95/46/EC. Article 10.1 provides that both countries will protect Personal Data furnished under this Agreement in accordance with the applicable provisions of the privacy and confidentiality laws of the country that receives the Personal Data.

[53] Article 10.2 provides that if either country modifies any of its statutes that regulate the privacy or confidentiality of Personal Data transmitted between the countries, the Competent Authority of the Contracting State that modified its statute must notify the Competent Authority of the other Contracting State.

[54] Article 10.3 protects a person's right to request particular information about any of his or her Personal Data requested from or transmitted to either country under this Agreement. Article 10.3 also provides that when a person requests such information about his or her Personal Data from a country, that country must provide the requested information to the person.

Authority's or Agency's request. In accordance with its respective national statutes, the receiving Competent Authority or Agency shall correct, limit access to, or delete any inaccurate or outdated transmitted Personal Data and any data not required to fulfill the receiving Agency's request, and immediately notify the other Contracting State's Competent Authority or Agency of such correction. This shall not limit a person's right to request such correction, limitation of access, or deletion of his or her Personal Data directly from the Agencies.[55]

5) Both the transmitting and the receiving Competent Authority or Agency shall effectively protect Personal Data against unauthorized or illegal access, alteration, or disclosure.[56]

Article 11: Confidentiality of Exchanged Employers' Information

Unless otherwise required by the national statutes of a Contracting State, employers' information transmitted between Contracting States in accordance with this Agreement shall be used exclusively for purposes of administering this Agreement and the Laws referred to in Article 2 of this Agreement. The receiving Contracting State's national statutes for the protection and confidentiality of employers' information, and the provisions of this Agreement generally, shall govern such use.[57]

---

[55] Article 10.4 provides that both countries will take reasonable steps to ensure the accuracy of Personal Data transmitted between the two countries and will limit the transmission of Personal Data to only that information necessary to satisfy the other country's request. However, if one country later discovers that it transmitted or received inaccurate or outdated Personal Data, or Personal Data not required to satisfy a country's request, the country that discovers the discrepancy will correct or delete the Personal Data in question and immediately notify the Agency of the other country. The countries will perform such correction or deletion in accordance with their respective statutes governing alteration and destruction of data.

Article 10.4 also recognizes the right of a person to ask either Agency directly to correct or delete any of his or her own Personal Data that he or she discovers to be inaccurate or not required to satisfy a Contracting State's request.

[56] Both the United States and Slovenia agree to protect the integrity, privacy, and confidentiality of Personal Data under their respective laws when receiving or transmitting such data under this Agreement.

[57] Article 11 provides protections for employers' confidential information. It provides to any business-related information exchanged under this Agreement similar protections to those provided for Personal Data under this Agreement and under each country's national statutes.

Article 12: Documents
1) Where the Laws of a Contracting State provide that any document which is submitted to the Competent Authority or an Agency of that Contracting State shall be exempted, wholly or partly, from fees or charges, including consular and administrative fees, the exemption shall also apply to corresponding documents which are submitted to the Competent Authority or an Agency of the other Contracting State in the application of this Agreement.[58]
2) Documents and certificates presented for purposes of this Agreement shall be exempted from requirements for authentication by diplomatic or consular authorities.[59]
3) Copies of documents certified as true and exact copies by an Agency of one Contracting State shall be accepted as true and exact copies by an Agency of the other Contracting State, without further certification. The Agency of each Contracting State shall be the final judge of the probative value of the evidence submitted to it from whatever source.[60]

Article 13: Correspondence and Language
1) The Competent Authorities and Agencies of the Contracting States may correspond directly with each other and with any person,

---

[58] Article 12.1 states that if the Laws of one country exempt documents submitted in connection with a social security claim from fees or charges, that exemption will also apply if a country sends such documents to the other country by or on behalf of a claimant or beneficiary.

[59] Some countries require that a diplomatic, consular, or other official representative in the other country certify the authenticity of documents submitted to their social security authorities by or on behalf of persons in another country. Both the United States and Slovenia are parties to the Hague Convention Abolishing the Requirement for Legalisation for Foreign Public Documents. Article 12.2 reaffirms that neither country will require such authentication of documents submitted under this Agreem.

[60] If the Agency of one country certifies that a copy of a document it furnishes to the Agency of the other country is a true and exact copy of an original document, the other country will accept this certification. Nevertheless, each country will remain the final judge of the probative value of any documents submitted to it under this Agreement.

wherever the person may reside, whenever it is necessary for the administration of this Agreement.[61]

2) An application or document may not be rejected by a Competent Authority or Agency of a Contracting State solely because it is in the language of the other Contracting State. If so needed, the Contracting States may agree to exchange model letters in the English or Slovenian language.[62]

Article 14: Applications

1) A written application for Benefits filed with an Agency of one Contracting State shall protect the rights of the claimants under the Laws of the other Contracting State if the applicant requests that it be considered an application under the Laws of the other Contracting State.[63]

2) If an applicant has filed a written application for Benefits with an Agency of one Contracting State and has not explicitly requested that the application be restricted to Benefits under the Laws of that Contracting State, the application shall also protect the rights of the claimants under the Laws of the other Contracting State if the applicant provides information at the time of filing indicating that the person on whose record Benefits are claimed has completed Periods of Coverage under the Laws of the other Contracting State.[64]

---

[61] Article 13.1 authorizes direct correspondence between the Competent Authorities and Agencies of the two countries and between these bodies and any person with whom they may need to communicate.

[62] The Competent Authorities and Agencies of each country may not reject an application or document because it is in the language of the other country. SSA already accepts applications and documents written in any language.
Article 13.2 also permits the Agencies of the two countries to exchange model letters in either language to facilitate the implementation of this Agreement.

[63] Under Article 14.1, a written application submitted to the Agency of one country that expresses intent to file for Benefits in the other country will protect the claimant's right to Benefits under the Laws of the other country as if the applicant presented it to the other country, provided the applicant expresses an intent to file for Benefits in the other country when filing the application.

[64] An applicant who files an application with the Agency of one country may not always know about his or her Benefit rights in the other country. Article 14.2 provides that even if it states no intention to file for Benefits in the other country, an application will also protect

3) The provisions of Part III of this Agreement shall apply only to Benefits for which an application is filed on or after the date on which this Agreement enters into force.[65]

Article 15: Appeals and Time Limits

1) A written appeal of a determination made by an Agency of one Contracting State may be validly filed with an Agency of either Contracting State. The appeal shall be decided according to the procedure and Laws of the Contracting State whose decision is being appealed.[66]
2) Any claim, notice, or written appeal which, under the Laws of one Contracting State, must have been filed within a prescribed period with an Agency of that Contracting State, but which is instead filed within the same period with an Agency of the other Contracting State, shall be considered to have been filed on time.[67]

Article 16: Transmittal of Claims, Notices, and Appeals

In any case to which the provisions of Article 14 or 15, or both, of this Agreement apply, the Agency to which the claim, notice, or written appeal has been submitted shall indicate the date of receipt on the document and transmit it without delay to the Liaison Agency of the other Contracting State.[68]

---

the claimant's rights under the other country's laws if the applicant indicates at the time of filing that the worker had coverage in the other country.

[65] Article 14.3 requires that a person claiming Benefits under this Agreement file an application on or after the date this Agreement enters into force.

[66] Both the United States and Slovenia have formal procedures for appealing the determinations of their Agencies. Under Article 15.1, a claimant may file a written appeal of a decision by the Agency of one country with the Agency of either country. The appropriate Agency of the country whose decision a person is appealing will consider the appeal under its own laws and procedures.

[67] Article 15.2 provides that when the Laws of one country require the submission of a claim, notice, or written appeal within a set time limit, the Agency of that country will consider it filed on time if the claimant files it with the Agency of the other country within that prescribed time limit.

[68] The Agency with which an applicant files a claim, notice, or written appeal under Article 14 or 15 of this Agreement shall transmit it immediately to the Liaison Agency of the other country. The sending Agency will indicate the date on which it received the document

Article 17: Currency
1) Payments under this Agreement may be made in the currency of the Contracting State making the payments.[69]
2) In case provisions designed to restrict the exchange or export of currencies are introduced by either Contracting State, the Governments of both Contracting States shall immediately take measures necessary to ensure the transfer of sums owed by either Contracting State under this Agreement.[70]

Article 18: Resolution of Disagreements
Any disagreement regarding the interpretation or application of this Agreement shall be resolved by consultation between the Competent Authorities.[71]

Article 19: Supplementary Agreements
This Agreement may be amended by supplementary Agreements.[72]

Part V. Transitional and Final Provisions

Article 20: Transitional Provisions
1) This Agreement shall not establish any claim to payment of a Benefit for any period before the date of entry into force of this Agreement, or to a lump sum death payment if the person died before the entry into force of this Agreement.[73]

---

[69] The Agencies may pay Benefits under this Agreement in the currency of either country. The United States pays Benefits abroad in U.S. dollars or, where possible, in the local currency. The IPII may pay Slovenian Benefits abroad in Euros.

[70] Should either country restrict the exchange of its currency, both Contracting States will take steps to ensure the payment of amounts due under the Agreement.

[71] Article 18 requires the Competent Authorities to attempt to resolve any dispute between them regarding this Agreement through consultation or negotiation.

[72] Article 19 provides that future supplementary agreements may amend this Agreement.

[73] The Agencies will pay Benefits based on the Agreement no earlier than the effective date of this Agreement. In addition, no person will be eligible to receive a lump-sum death payment if the worker died prior to the entry into force of this Agreement.

2) In determining the right to Benefits under this Agreement, consideration shall be given to Periods of Coverage under the Laws of both Contracting States and other events that occurred before the entry into force of this Agreement.[74]

3) In applying paragraphs 2, 3, 4 or 5 of Article 5 of this Agreement in the case of persons who were sent to work by their employer or transferred their self-employment activity to the territory of a Contracting State prior to the date of entry into force of this Agreement, the period of employment or self-employment shall be considered to begin on the date of entry into force of this Agreement.[75]

4) Determinations concerning entitlement to Benefits made before the entry into force of this Agreement shall not affect rights arising under it.[76]

5) The application of this Agreement shall not result in any reduction in the amount of a Benefit to which entitlement was established prior to the entry into force of this Agreement.[77]

---

[74] In determining Benefit eligibility and amounts under this Agreement, Article 20.2 provides that the Agencies will consider Periods of Coverage earned before this Agreement enters into force. The Agencies will also consider events relevant to the determination of Benefit rights, such as marriage, death, disability, or attainment of a certain age, which happened prior to this Agreement's effective date.
However, the United States will not consider Slovenian Periods of Coverage credited prior to 1937, the earliest date for which U.S. Laws permit crediting Periods of Coverage. (See Article 6.4). Additionally, the United States will not pay a lump sum death payment under this Agreement if the person on whose record a claimant files for Benefits died prior to this Agreement's entry into force. (See Article 20.1).

[75] Article 20.3 provides that the Agencies will measure the 5-year period to which paragraphs 2, 3, 4, and 5 of Article 5 refer beginning no earlier than the date this Agreement enters into force. Thus, for persons to whom these provisions apply who were working in the other country before this Agreement's effective date, the prior period will not count for purposes of the 5-year limit.

[76] A decision to award or deny a claim either Agency renders prior to the effective date of this Agreement will not prevent a person from filing a new application for other Benefits that may be payable because of this Agreement.

[77] Article 20.5 guarantees that the entry into force of this Agreement will not result in a reduction in Benefits already payable at the time this Agreement becomes effective.

Article 21: Duration and Termination
1) This Agreement shall remain in force until the expiration of one (1) calendar year following the year in which written notice of its

termination is given by one of the Contracting States to the other Contracting State.[78]

2) If this Agreement is terminated, rights regarding entitlement to or payment of Benefits acquired under it shall be retained, and any claim filed, but not adjudicated, before the termination of this Agreement shall be adjudicated in accordance with the provisions of this Agreement.[79]

Article 22: Entry into Force

This Agreement shall enter into force on the first day of the fourth month following the date of the last note of an exchange of diplomatic notes in which the Contracting States notify each other of the completion of their respective internal procedures necessary for the entry into force of this Agreement.[80]

IN WITNESS WHEREOF, the undersigned, being duly authorized thereto, have signed the present Agreement.

DONE at Ljubljana this 17th day of January, 2017, in duplicate in the English and Slovenian languages, both texts being equally authentic. [81]

For The United States of America:
Brent R. Hartley
For The Republic of Slovenia:
Anja Kopač Mrak

---

[78] Either country can terminate this Agreement by giving written notice of termination to the other. If either country takes actions to terminate this Agreement, it will remain in effect until the expiration of one (1) calendar year after the year in which one of the countries receives written notice of termination from the other.

[79] If either country terminates this Agreement, a person will retain Benefit rights acquired before termination. In addition, if any person files a claim prior to this Agreement's termination, the Agency of the country under whose Laws the person is applying for Benefits will adjudicate the claim in accordance with the provisions of this Agreement, even if such adjudication will be made after the termination of this Agreement.

[80] Once each country completes its internal approval process, the two governments will exchange formal instruments of approval. This Agreement will enter into force on the first day of the fourth calendar month after the month in which each government receives notification of approval from the other government.

[81] The U.S. Ambassador to Slovenia, Brent R. Hartley, and the Slovenian Minister of Labour, Family, Social Affairs and Equal Opportunities, Anja Kopač Mrak, signed this Agreement on January 17, 2017 in Ljubljana.

Administrative Arrangement Between the United States of America and the Republic of Slovenia for the Implementation of the Agreement on Social Security Between the United States of America and the Republic of Slovenia

The United States of America and the Republic of Slovenia, In conformity with Article 8(a) of the Agreement on Social Security between the United States of America and the Republic of Slovenia of this date, hereinafter referred to as the "Agreement," have agreed as follows:

Chapter I. General Provisions

Article 1

Where terms that appear in the Agreement are used in this Administrative Arrangement, they shall have the same meaning as they have in the Agreement.[82]

Article 2

1) The Liaison Agencies referred to in Article 8(a) of the Agreement shall be:
   a) for the United States of America, the Social Security Administration; and
   b) for the Republic of Slovenia,
      i. for the Laws referred to under Article 2, paragraph 1, subparagraph (b)(i) of the Agreement: the Pension and Disability Insurance Institute of Slovenia, and
      ii. for the Laws referred to under Article 2, paragraph 1, subparagraph (b)(ii) of the Agreement: the Health Insurance Institute of Slovenia.[83]

---

[82] Article 1 provides that terms have the same meaning in this Administrative Arrangement as they do in the Agreement.

2) The Liaison Agencies designated in paragraph 1 of this Article shall decide upon the joint procedures, methods, and bilingual forms necessary for the implementation of the Agreement and this Administrative Arrangement. [84]

Chapter II. Provisions on Coverage

Article 3

1) Where the Laws of one Contracting State are applicable in accordance with any of the provisions of Article 5 of the Agreement, the Agency of that Contracting State, upon request of the employer or self-employed person, shall issue a certificate stating that the employee or self-employed person is subject to those Laws and indicating the duration for which the certificate shall be valid. This certificate shall be evidence that the employee or self-employed person is exempt from the Laws on compulsory coverage of the other Contracting State.[85]

2) The certificate referred to in paragraph 1 of this Article shall be issued[86]:

---

[83] Article 2.1 designates the Liaison Agencies in each country responsible for implementing and administering the coverage and Benefit provisions of the Agreement. The United States designates the Social Security Administration as its Liaison Agency, and the Republic of Slovenia ("Slovenia") designates the Pension and Disability Insurance Institute of Slovenia and the Health Insurance Institute of Slovenia as its counterpart Liaison Agencies for purposes of Benefits and coverage issues, respectively.

[84] Article 2.2 authorizes and requires the Liaison Agencies of both countries to agree upon those procedures, methods and forms they will use for the implementation of the Agreement and this Administrative Arrangement.

[85] Under Article 3.1, the Agency of the country whose social security coverage Laws will continue to apply to a person in accordance with the rules in Part II of the Agreement will issue a certificate to that effect when an employer or a self-employed person requests one. Employers and self-employed persons should request certificates before work begins in the other country, whenever possible. The certificate will serve as evidence of the exemption of the person from the coverage Laws of the other country when provided to the Agency of the other country.

[86] Article 3.3 provides that the Agency issuing a coverage certificate will furnish a copy of the certificate or information from the certificate to the Liaison Agency in the other country when needed.

a) in the United States, by the Social Security Administration; and

b) in the Republic of Slovenia, by the Health Insurance Institute of Slovenia.

3) The Agency of a Contracting State that issues a certificate referred to in paragraph 1 of this Article shall furnish a copy of the certificate or mutually decided information from the certificate to the Liaison Agency of the other Contracting State as needed by the Agency of the other Contracting State.[87]

4) The Competent Authorities referred to in paragraph 8 of Article 5 of the Agreement shall be[88]:

a) for the United States of America, the Commissioner of Social Security; and

b) for the Republic of Slovenia, the Ministry of Labor, Family, Social Affairs, and Equal Opportunities.

Chapter III. Provisions on Benefits

Article 4

1) Claims for Benefits under the Agreement shall be submitted on forms to be developed by the Liaison Agencies of the two Contracting States.[89]

---

[87] Article 3.3 provides that the Agency issuing a coverage certificate will furnish a copy of the certificate or information from the certificate to the Liaison Agency in the other country when needed.

[88] Article 3.4, added at the behest of the Slovenian delegation, designates the Slovenian Competent Authority for purposes of granting exceptions to the normal coverage rules of the Agreement as provided in Article 5.8 of the Agreement. Since the Health Insurance Institute of Slovenia will share a joint role as Competent Authority with the Ministry of Labor, Family, Social Affairs, and Equal Opportunities, this provision makes clear that only the Ministry of Labour, Family, Social Affairs, and Equal Opportunities can grant such exceptions described in Article 5.8 of the Agreement. For the United States, the Competent Authority remains the Commissioner of Social Security.

[89] The U.S. and Slovenian Liaison Agencies will agree on special application forms that people who wish to file for Benefits based on the Agreement will use.

2) The Agency of the Contracting State with which a claim for Benefits is first filed in accordance with Article 14 of the Agreement, shall provide the Agency of the other Contracting State with such evidence and other information in its possession as may be required to complete action on the claim.[90]

3) The Agency of a Contracting State which receives a claim that was first filed with an Agency of the other Contracting State, shall without delay provide the Agency of the other Contracting State with such evidence and other available information in its possession as may be required for it to complete action on the claim.

4) The Agency of the Contracting State with which a claim for Benefits has been filed shall verify the information pertaining to the applicant and the applicant's family members. The Liaison Agencies of both Contracting States shall decide upon the types of information to be verified.[91]

5) Upon request, the Agency of one Contracting State shall inform the Agency of the other Contracting State on bilingual forms of its decision to award or deny a claim filed under Part III of the Agreement.[92]

---

[90] Articles 4.2 and 4.3 outline the procedures both countries will follow for the exchange of evidence and information they need to process claims filed under the Agreement.

[91] Article 4.4 deals with the verification of claims information. Both U.S. and Slovenian Laws require verification of certain information about people claiming Benefits (e.g., age and family relationship to the worker) before either country can approve the claim. Article 4.4 provides that when a person files a claim for Benefits under the Agreement in one country, the Agency of that country will verify the relevant information and inform the Liaison Agency of the other country of its findings. The Liaison Agencies will agree upon the specific types of information requiring verification. This provision expedites the claims process by avoiding duplicate verification of the same information. An Agency may still request additional evidence to support the finding of the other Agency.

[92] Article 4.5 requires an Agency, upon request of the other country's Agency, to notify the Agency of the other country of its decision pertaining to the award or denial of Benefits with respect to any specific person. Such notification will be carried out on bilingual liaison forms to be developed at a later implementation meeting between the two Liaison Agencies.

Chapter IV. Miscellaneous Provisions

Article 5
1) In accordance with measures to be decided upon pursuant to paragraph 2 of Article 2 of this Administrative Arrangement, the Agency of one Contracting State shall, upon request by the Agency of the other Contracting State, furnish available information relating to the claim of any specified individual for the purpose of administering the Agreement.[93]
2) For the purpose of facilitation of the implementation of the Agreement and this Administrative Arrangement, the Liaison Agencies may decide on measures for the provision and transmission of the electronic exchange of data.[94]

Article 6
The Liaison Agencies shall exchange statistics on the number of certificates issued under Article 3 of this Administrative Arrangement and on the payments made to beneficiaries under the Agreement. These statistics shall be furnished annually in a manner to be decided upon by the Liaison Agencies.[95]

Article 7
1) Where administrative assistance is requested and provided under Article 9 of the Agreement, expenses other than regular personnel and operating costs of the Agency providing the assistance shall be reimbursed, except as may be otherwise agreed to by the

---

[93] Article 5.1 provides that the Agency of one country will, upon request, furnish claims related information to the Agency of the other country in accordance with agreed upon procedures. Such procedures will be decided upon by the Agencies and will be consistent with the governing statutes of both countries.
[94] Under Article 5.2, the Liaison Agencies of both countries may choose to implement electronic data exchanges to facilitate administration of the Agreement and this Administrative Arrangement. Such exchanges must comply with the laws of each country governing the protection of privacy and confidentiality of Personal Data.
[95] Article 6 provides for an exchange of statistics concerning certificates issued pursuant to Article 3.1 of this Administrative Arrangement and payments made to beneficiaries under the Agreement.

Competent Authorities or Liaison Agencies of the Contracting States.[96]

2) Upon request, the Agency of either Contracting State shall furnish without cost to the Agency of the other Contracting State any medical information and documentation in its possession relevant to the disability of the claimant or beneficiary.[97]

3) Where the Agency of a Contracting State requires that a person in the territory of the other Contracting State who is receiving or applying for Benefits under the Agreement submit to a medical examination, such examination, if requested by that Agency, shall be arranged by the Agency of the other Contracting State in accordance with the rules of the Agency making the arrangements and at the expense of the Agency requesting the examination.[98]

4) The Agency of one Contracting State shall reimburse amounts owed under paragraphs 1 or 3 of this Article upon presentation of a statement of expenses by the Agency of the other Contracting State.[99]

---

[96] In accordance with Article 9 of the Agreement, the Agencies of the two countries will provide each other with administrative assistance required to implement the Agreement. Under Article 7.1, the requesting Agency will pay expenses the other Agency incurs in responding to requests for administrative assistance that require it to go outside its own organization unless the two countries agree on a different arrangement. This includes hiring interpreters, conducting special field investigations, or arranging medical examinations. The Agencies will not reimburse expenses for regular personnel and operating costs.

[97] When the Agency in one country requests medical information from the Agency in the other country, the other Agency will provide the requesting Agency with any pertinent medical records it has in its possession free of charge.

[98] Article 7.3 provides that where a medical examination is necessary to establish eligibility for or continuing entitlement to a country's Benefits that are payable under the Agreement, and the claimant or beneficiary is in the other country, the Agency of the other country, upon request, will arrange for the examination at the expense of the Agency requesting the examination.

[99] In order to receive reimbursement for the cost of administrative assistance, the Agency that provides the assistance must provide the requesting Agency with a statement of expenses.

Article 8
1) The Agency shall pay Benefits directly to the beneficiary or his or her designee.[100]
2) Upon request of the Agency referred to in paragraph 1 of this Article, a beneficiary shall submit proof, annually at minimum, that he or she is still alive.[101]

Article 9

The Competent Authorities shall notify each other, in writing, of changes in the names of the Liaison Agencies without the need to modify the Administrative Arrangement.[102]

Article 10

This Administrative Arrangement shall enter into force on the date of entry into force of the Agreement and remain in force so long as the Agreement is in force.[103]

DONE at Ljubljana, this 17th day of January, 2017, in duplicate in the English and Slovenian languages, both texts being equally authentic.[104]

For the United States of America: Brent R. Hartley

For the Republic of Slovenia: Anja Kopač Mrak

---

[100] Article 8.1 provides that both countries will only pay Benefits under the Agreement to either the beneficiary or a legally appointed designee of the beneficiary.
[101] Slovenia requested the inclusion of this provision. Under Article 8.2, an Agency making payments under the Agreement shall be able to request evidence and other information from a beneficiary indicating that he or she is alive.
[102] Article 9 provides that changes to the names of the Liaison Agencies will not require the two sides to modify this Administrative Arrangement.
[103] This Administrative Arrangement will enter into force on the same date as the Agreement and will remain in effect for the same period as the Agreement.
[104] The U.S. Ambassador to Slovenia, Brent R. Hartley, and the Slovenian Minister of Labour, Family, Social Affairs and Equal Opportunities, Anja Kopac Mrak, signed this Administrative Arrangement on January 17, 2017 in Ljubljana.

AGREEMENT ON SOCIAL SECURITY BETWEEN THE UNITED STATES OF AMERICA AND THE REPUBLIC OF SLOVENIA

The United States of America and The Republic of Slovenia (hereinafter individually known as "Contracting State" or collectively as "Contracting States"), Being desirous of regulating the relationship between the two countries in the field of social security, have agreed as follows:

Part I. General Provisions

Article 1: Definitions

1) For the purposes of the Agreement on Social Security between the United States of America and the Republic of Slovenia (hereinafter "Agreement"):
   a) "National" means,
      as regards the United States, a national of the United States as defined in Section 101, Immigration and Nationality Act, as amended, and
      as regards the Republic of Slovenia, a national of the Republic of Slovenia as defined in the Citizenship of the Republic of Slovenia Act, as amended;
   b) "Laws" means the laws and regulations specified in Article 2 of this Agreement;
   c) "Competent Authority" means,
      as regards the United States, the Commissioner of Social Security, and
      as regards the Republic of Slovenia, the competent ministries with the powers conferred by the legislative acts defined in Article 2 of this Agreement;
   d) "Agency" means,

as regards the United States, the Social Security Administration, and

as regards the Republic of Slovenia, the institutions, funds and bodies, responsible for the implementation of the Laws defined in Article 2, Paragraph 1, subparagraph b of this Agreement;

e) "Period of Coverage" means a period of payment of contributions or a period of earnings from employment or self-employment, as defined or recognized as a period of coverage by the Laws under which such period has been completed, or any similar period in-so-far as it is recognized by such Laws as equivalent to a period of coverage;

f) "Benefit" means any benefit provided for in the Laws specified in Article 2 of this Agreement;

g) "Personal Data" means any information relating to a specific (identified or identifiable) person, as well as any information that can be used to distinguish or trace an individual's identity. This includes, but is not limited to, the following: any individual identifier; citizenship, nationality, statelessness, or refugee status; benefits, eligibility, or other claims information; contact information; medical information or lay information used in a medical determination; information about marital, familial, or personal relationships; and information pertaining to work, financial, or economic status; and

h) "Liaison Agencies" means institutions authorized to route inquiries and correspondence for effective implementation of this Agreement.

2) Any term not defined in this Article shall have the meaning assigned to it in the applicable Laws.

Article 2: Material Scope

1) For the purposes of this Agreement, the applicable Laws are:

a) as regards the United States, the laws governing the Federal old-age, survivors, and disability insurance program:
   i. Title II of the Social Security Act and regulations pertaining thereto, except sections 226, 226A, and 228 of that title, and regulations pertaining to those sections, and
   ii. Chapters 2 and 21 of the Internal Revenue Code of 1986 and regulations pertaining to those chapters; and
b) as regards the Republic of Slovenia:
   i. the laws governing pension and disability insurance, except the provisions on residual working capacity, and
   ii. with regard to Part II of this Agreement only, the laws of the Republic of Slovenia governing the compulsory participation in social insurance system.

2) Unless otherwise provided in this Agreement, the Laws referred to in paragraph 1 of this Article shall not include treaties or other international agreements or supranational legislation on Social Security concluded between one Contracting State and a third State, or laws or regulations promulgated for their specific implementation.

3) No provision in this Agreement shall affect the obligation of either Contracting State's social security agreements or any other international agreements by which either Contracting State is bound.

4) Except as provided in the following sentence, this Agreement shall also apply to laws and regulations that amend or supplement the Laws specified in paragraph 1 of this Article. This Agreement shall apply to future laws and regulations of a Contracting State which create new categories of beneficiaries or new Benefits under the Laws of that Contracting State unless the Competent Authority of that Contracting State notifies the Competent Authority of the other Contracting State in writing within three (3) months of the date of the official publication of the new laws or regulations that no such extension of this Agreement is intended.

Article 3: Persons Covered

This Agreement shall apply:

a) to any person who is or has been subject to the Laws of either Contracting State, and
b) to the dependents and survivors of a person described in subparagraph (a) of this Article within the meaning of the applicable Laws of either Contracting State.

Article 4: Equality of Treatment

1) Unless otherwise provided in this Agreement, persons described in Article 3 of this Agreement who reside in the territory of one Contracting State shall receive equal treatment with Nationals of the second Contracting State in the application of the Laws of the second Contracting State.
2) Unless otherwise provided in this Agreement, any provision of the Laws of a Contracting State which restricts entitlement to or payment of Benefits solely because a person resides outside or is absent from the territory of that Contracting State shall not be applicable to a person who resides in the territory of the other Contracting State.

Part II. Provisions Concerning Applicable Laws

Article 5: Coverage Provisions

1) Except as otherwise provided in this Article, a person employed or self-employed within the territory of one of the Contracting States, with respect to that employment or self-employment, shall be subject to the Laws of only that Contracting State.
2) Where a person who is normally employed in the territory of one Contracting State by an employer in that territory is sent by that employer to the territory of the other Contracting State for a

temporary period that is not expected to exceed five (5) years, the person shall be subject to the Laws of only the first Contracting State as if the person were employed in the territory of the first Contracting State.

3) For purposes of applying paragraph 2 of this Article in the case of an employee who is sent from the territory of the United States by an employer in that territory to the territory of the Republic of Slovenia, that employer and an affiliated company of the employer (as defined under the laws of the United States) shall be considered one and the same, provided that the employment would have been covered under United States Laws absent this Agreement.

4) Paragraphs 2 and 3 of this Article shall apply where a person who has been sent by his or her employer from the territory of a Contracting State to the territory of a third State, and who is compulsorily covered under the Laws of that Contracting State while employed in the territory of the third State, is subsequently sent by that employer from the territory of the third State to the territory of the other Contracting State.

5) A person who is normally self-employed in the territory of one Contracting State, and who temporarily transfers his or her self-employment activity to the territory of the other Contracting State shall be subject to the Laws of only the first Contracting State, provided that the period of self-employment activity in the territory of the other Contracting State is not expected to exceed five (5) years.

6) (a) A person who is employed as an officer or member of a crew on a vessel which flies the flag of one Contracting State and who would be covered under the Laws of both Contracting States shall be subject to the Laws of only the Contracting State whose flag the vessel flies. For purposes of the preceding sentence, a vessel which flies the flag of the United States is one defined as an American vessel under the Laws of the United States.

(b) Traveling employees of air transportation companies who perform work in the territories of both Contracting States and who would otherwise be covered under the Laws of both Contracting States shall, with respect to that work, be subject to the Laws of only the Contracting State in the territory of which the company has its headquarters. However, if such employees reside in the territory of the other Contracting State, they shall be subject to the Laws of only that Contracting State.

7) (a) This Agreement shall not affect the provisions of the Vienna Convention on Diplomatic Relations of April 18, 1961, or of the Vienna Convention on Consular Relations of April 24, 1963.

(b) Nationals of one of the Contracting States who are employed by the Government of that Contracting State in the territory of the other Contracting State but who are not exempt from the Laws of the other Contracting State by virtue of the Vienna Conventions mentioned in subparagraph (a) of this paragraph shall be subject to the Laws of only the first Contracting State. For the purpose of this paragraph, employment by the United States Government includes employment by an instrumentality thereof.

8) The Competent Authorities of the two Contracting States may agree to grant an exception to the provisions of this Article with respect to particular persons or categories of persons, provided that any affected person shall be subject to the Laws of one of the Contracting States.

Part III. Provisions on Benefits

Article 6: United States Benefits

1) Where a person has completed at least six (6) quarters of coverage under United States Laws, but does not have sufficient Periods of Coverage to satisfy the requirements for entitlement to Benefits under United States Laws, the Agency of the United States shall take into account, for the purpose of establishing entitlement to Benefits under this Article, Periods of Coverage which are credited under Republic of Slovenia Laws and which do not coincide with Periods of Coverage already credited under United States Laws.

2) In determining eligibility for Benefits under paragraph 1 of this Article, the Agency of the United States shall credit one (1) quarter of coverage for every ninety (90) days of coverage certified by the Agency of the Republic of Slovenia. The total number of quarters of coverage to be credited for a year shall not exceed four (4).

3) Where it is not possible to determine the calendar quarter during which a specific Period of Coverage was completed under the Laws of the United States, the United States Agency will presume that the Period of Coverage does not coincide with a Period of Coverage completed in the Republic of Slovenia.

4) The Agency of the United States shall not take into account Periods of Coverage that occurred prior to the earliest date for which Periods of Coverage may be credited under its Laws, nor will the Agency of the United States take into account any Periods of Coverage that are not based on paid contributions.

5) Where entitlement to a Benefit under United States Laws is established according to the provisions of paragraph 1 of this Article, the Agency of the United States shall compute a pro rata Primary Insurance Amount in accordance with United States Laws based on
    a) the person's average earnings credited exclusively under United States Laws and
    b) the ratio of the duration of the person's Periods of Coverage completed under United States Laws to the duration of a coverage lifetime as determined in accordance with United States Laws.

Benefits payable under United States Laws shall be based on the pro rata Primary Insurance Amount.

6) Entitlement to a Benefit from the United States that results from paragraph 1 of this Article shall terminate with the acquisition of sufficient Periods of Coverage under United States Laws to

establish entitlement to an equal or higher Benefit without the need to invoke the provision of paragraph 1 of this Article.
7) Article 4 of this Agreement shall be applied by the United States in a manner consistent with section 233(c)(4) of the United States Social Security Act.

Article 7: Republic of Slovenia Benefits

1) Where the requirements for entitlement to Benefits under Republic of Slovenia Laws are satisfied without the Periods of Coverage under United States Laws, the Republic of Slovenia Agency shall provide Benefits for the Periods of Coverage exclusively completed under Republic of Slovenia Laws.
2) Where the requirements for entitlements to Benefits under Republic of Slovenia Laws are not satisfied on the basis of Periods of Coverage completed under Republic of Slovenia Laws alone, the Republic of Slovenia Agency shall take into account, for the purpose of establishing entitlements to Benefits, Periods of Coverage which are credited under United States Laws and do not coincide with Periods of Coverage credited under Republic of Slovenia Laws.
3) Where entitlement requirements under paragraph 2 of this Article are not satisfied, the Republic of Slovenia Agency shall also take into account the periods completed under the Laws of third countries with which the Republic of Slovenia has concluded international Social Security Agreements with provisions on the totalization of periods.
4) When entitlement to Benefits is established through procedures referred to in paragraphs 2 and 3 of this Article, the Republic of Slovenia Agency shall calculate the Benefit amount as follows:
    a) First, a theoretical amount of the Benefit which would be paid if all the totalized Periods of Coverage were completed under Republic of Slovenia Laws, is calculated.
    b) The theoretical amount is then used for the calculation of the actual amount of the Benefit to be paid in the proportional

relation to the Period of Coverage completed under Republic of Slovenia Laws and other Periods of Coverage used for the purposes of totalization.
   c) The calculation of the theoretical amount of the Benefit referred to in subparagraph (a) of this paragraph for the purposes of the determination of the Benefit shall only take into account Periods of Coverage completed under the Republic of Slovenia Laws.
5) When establishing the entitlement to Benefits referred to in paragraphs 2 and 3 of this Article, the Republic of Slovenia Agency shall equal each quarter reported by the United States Agency to a Period of Coverage of three (3) months.
6) Where the total Periods of Coverage completed under Republic of Slovenia Laws amount to less than twelve (12) months, the Benefit shall not be granted. This provision does not apply if – under Republic of Slovenia Laws – the entitlement to Benefit exists solely on the basis of such a short Period of Coverage.
7) Assistance and Attendance Allowance, Disability Allowance, Residual Working Capacity Benefit or any other noncontributory benefit which is not exportable under Republic of Slovenia Laws, shall be paid as long as the beneficiary resides in the territory of the Republic of Slovenia.

Part IV. Miscellaneous Provisions

Article 8: Administrative Arrangements
   The Contracting States shall:

   a) make all necessary administrative arrangements for the implementation of this Agreement and designate Liaison Agencies;
   b) communicate to each other information concerning the measures taken for the application of this Agreement; and

c) communicate to each other, as soon as possible, information concerning all changes in their respective Laws which may affect the application of this Agreement.

Article 9: Mutual Assistance

The Competent Authorities and the Agencies of the Contracting States, within the scope of their respective authorities, shall assist each other in implementing this Agreement. This assistance shall be free of charge, subject to exceptions to be agreed upon in an administrative arrangement.

Article 10: Confidentiality of Exchanged Personal Data

1) Unless otherwise required by the national statutes of a Contracting State, Personal Data transmitted in accordance with this Agreement to one Contracting State by the other Contracting State shall be used exclusively for purposes of administering this Agreement and the Laws referred to in Article 2 of this Agreement. The receiving Contracting State's national statutes for the protection of privacy and confidentiality of Personal Data, and the provisions of this Agreement generally, shall govern such use.

2) The Competent Authorities of the Contracting States shall inform each other about all amendments to their national statutes regarding the protection of privacy and confidentiality of Personal Data that affect the transmission of Personal Data.

3) The Competent Authority or Agency requesting or transmitting Personal Data pursuant to this Agreement, upon request, must disclose to a person the following:
   a) the content of his or her Personal Data,
   b) the Agency receiving his or her Personal Data,
   c) the duration of use of his or her Personal Data, and
   d) the purpose and legal grounds for which his or her Personal Data were used or requested.

4) The Competent Authority or Agency transmitting Personal Data pursuant to this Agreement shall, subject to the information available to the transmitting Contracting State, take all reasonable

steps to ensure that transmitted Personal Data are accurate, up to date and limited to data required to fulfill the receiving Competent Authority's or Agency's request. In accordance with its respective national statutes, the receiving Competent Authority or Agency shall correct, limit access to, or delete any inaccurate or outdated transmitted Personal Data and any data not required to fulfill the receiving Agency's request, and immediately notify the other Contracting State's Competent Authority or Agency of such correction. This shall not limit a person's right to request such correction, limitation of access, or deletion of his or her Personal Data directly from the Agencies.
5) Both the transmitting and the receiving Competent Authority or Agency shall effectively protect Personal Data against unauthorized or illegal access, alteration, or disclosure.

Article 11: Confidentiality of Exchanged Employers' Information

Unless otherwise required by the national statutes of a Contracting State, employers' information transmitted between Contracting States in accordance with this Agreement shall be used exclusively for purposes of administering this Agreement and the Laws referred to in Article 2 of this Agreement. The receiving Contracting State's national statutes for the protection and confidentiality of employers' information, and the provisions of this Agreement generally, shall govern such use.

Article 12: Documents

1) Where the Laws of a Contracting State provide that any document which is submitted to the Competent Authority or an Agency of that Contracting State shall be exempted, wholly or partly, from fees or charges, including consular and administrative fees, the exemption shall also apply to corresponding documents which are submitted to the Competent Authority or an Agency of the other Contracting State in the application of this Agreement.

2) Documents and certificates presented for purposes of this Agreement shall be exempted from requirements for authentication by diplomatic or consular authorities.
3) Copies of documents certified as true and exact copies by an Agency of one Contracting State shall be accepted as true and exact copies by an Agency of the other Contracting State, without further certification. The Agency of each Contracting State shall be the final judge of the probative value of the evidence submitted to it from whatever source.

Article 13: Correspondence and Language
1) The Competent Authorities and Agencies of the Contracting States may correspond directly with each other and with any person, wherever the person may reside, whenever it is necessary for the administration of this Agreement.
2) An application or document may not be rejected by a Competent Authority or Agency of a Contracting State solely because it is in the language of the other Contracting State. If so needed, the Contracting States may agree to exchange model letters in the English or Slovenian language.

Article 14: Applications
1) A written application for Benefits filed with an Agency of one Contracting State shall protect the rights of the claimants under the Laws of the other Contracting State if the applicant requests that it be considered an application under the Laws of the other Contracting State.
2) If an applicant has filed a written application for Benefits with an Agency of one Contracting State and has not explicitly requested that the application be restricted to Benefits under the Laws of that Contracting State, the application shall also protect the rights of the claimants under the Laws of the other Contracting State if the applicant provides information at the time of filing indicating that

the person on whose record Benefits are claimed has completed Periods of Coverage under the Laws of the other Contracting State.
3) The provisions of Part III of this Agreement shall apply only to Benefits for which an application is filed on or after the date on which this Agreement enters into force.

Article 15: Appeals and Time Limits
1) A written appeal of a determination made by an Agency of one Contracting State may be validly filed with an Agency of either Contracting State. The appeal shall be decided according to the procedure and Laws of the Contracting State whose decision is being appealed.
2) Any claim, notice, or written appeal which, under the Laws of one Contracting State, must have been filed within a prescribed period with an Agency of that Contracting State, but which is instead filed within the same period with an Agency of the other Contracting State, shall be considered to have been filed on time.

Article 16: Transmittal of Claims, Notices, and Appeals
In any case to which the provisions of Article 14 or 15, or both, of this Agreement apply, the Agency to which the claim, notice, or written appeal has been submitted shall indicate the date of receipt on the document and transmit it without delay to the Liaison Agency of the other Contracting State.

Article 17: Currency
1) Payments under this Agreement may be made in the currency of the Contracting State making the payments.
2) In case provisions designed to restrict the exchange or export of currencies are introduced by either Contracting State, the Governments of both Contracting States shall immediately take measures necessary to ensure the transfer of sums owed by either Contracting State under this Agreement.

Article 18: Resolution of Disagreements

Any disagreement regarding the interpretation or application of this Agreement shall be resolved by consultation between the Competent Authorities.

Article 19: Supplementary Agreements

This Agreement may be amended by supplementary Agreements.

Part V. Transitional and Final Provisions

Article 20: Transitional Provisions
1) This Agreement shall not establish any claim to payment of a Benefit for any period before the date of entry into force of this Agreement, or to a lump sum death payment if the person died before the entry into force of this Agreement.
2) In determining the right to Benefits under this Agreement, consideration shall be given to Periods of Coverage under the Laws of both Contracting States and other events that occurred before the entry into force of this Agreement.
3) In applying paragraphs 2, 3, 4 or 5 of Article 5 of this Agreement in the case of persons who were sent to work by their employer or transferred their self-employment activity to the territory of a Contracting State prior to the date of entry into force of this Agreement, the period of employment or self-employment shall be considered to begin on the date of entry into force of this Agreement.
4) Determinations concerning entitlement to Benefits made before the entry into force of this Agreement shall not affect rights arising under it.
5) The application of this Agreement shall not result in any reduction in the amount of a Benefit to which entitlement was established prior to the entry into force of this Agreement.

Article 21: Duration and Termination
1) This Agreement shall remain in force until the expiration of one (1) calendar year following the year in which written notice of its termination is given by one of the Contracting States to the other Contracting State.
2) If this Agreement is terminated, rights regarding entitlement to or payment of Benefits acquired under it shall be retained, and any claim filed, but not adjudicated, before the termination of this Agreement shall be adjudicated in accordance with the provisions of this Agreement.

Article 22: Entry into Force

This Agreement shall enter into force on the first day of the fourth month following the date of the last note of an exchange of diplomatic notes in which the Contracting States notify each other of the completion of their respective internal procedures necessary for the entry into force of this Agreement.

IN WITNESS WHEREOF, the undersigned, being duly authorized thereto, have signed the present Agreement.

DONE at Ljubljana this 17th day of January, 2017, in duplicate in the English and Slovenian languages, both texts being equally authentic.

For the United States of America: Brent R. Hartley

For the Republic of Slovenia: Anja Kopač Mrak

ADMINISTRATIVE ARRANGEMENT BETWEEN THE UNITED STATES OF AMERICA AND THE REPUBLIC OF SLOVENIA FOR THE IMPLEMENTATION OF THE AGREEMENT ON SOCIAL SECURITY BETWEEN THE UNITED STATES OF AMERICA AND THE REPUBLIC OF SLOVENIA

The United States of America and the Republic of Slovenia, In conformity with Article 8(a) of the Agreement on Social Security between the United States of America and the Republic of Slovenia of this date, hereinafter referred to as the "Agreement," have agreed as follows:

Chapter I. General Provisions

Article 1

Where terms that appear in the Agreement are used in this Administrative Arrangement, they shall have the same meaning as they have in the Agreement.

Article 2
1) The Liaison Agencies referred to in Article 8(a) of the Agreement shall be:
   a) for the United States of America, the Social Security Administration; and
   b) for the Republic of Slovenia,
      i. for the Laws referred to under Article 2, paragraph 1, subparagraph (b)(i) of the Agreement: the Pension and Disability Insurance Institute of Slovenia, and
      ii. for the Laws referred to under Article 2, paragraph 1, subparagraph (b)(ii) of the Agreement: the Health Insurance Institute of Slovenia.
2) The Liaison Agencies designated in paragraph 1 of this Article shall decide upon the joint procedures, methods, and bilingual forms necessary for the implementation of the Agreement and this Administrative Arrangement.

Chapter II. Provisions on Coverage

Article 3

1) Where the Laws of one Contracting State are applicable in accordance with any of the provisions of Article 5 of the

Agreement, the Agency of that Contracting State, upon request of the employer or self-employed person, shall issue a certificate stating that the employee or self-employed person is subject to those Laws and indicating the duration for which the certificate shall be valid. This certificate shall be evidence that the employee or self-employed person is exempt from the Laws on compulsory coverage of the other Contracting State.

2) The certificate referred to in paragraph 1 of this Article shall be issued:
   a) in the United States, by the Social Security Administration; and
   b) in the Republic of Slovenia, by the Health Insurance Institute of Slovenia.

3) The Agency of a Contracting State that issues a certificate referred to in paragraph 1 of this Article shall furnish a copy of the certificate or mutually decided information from the certificate to the Liaison Agency of the other Contracting State as needed by the Agency of the other Contracting State.

4) The Competent Authorities referred to in paragraph 8 of Article 5 of the Agreement shall be:
   a) for the United States of America, the Commissioner of Social Security; and
   b) for the Republic of Slovenia, the Ministry of Labor, Family, Social Affairs, and Equal Opportunities.

Chapter III. Provisions on Benefits

Article 4

1) Claims for Benefits under the Agreement shall be submitted on forms to be developed by the Liaison Agencies of the two Contracting States.
2) The Agency of the Contracting State with which a claim for Benefits is first filed in accordance with Article 14 of the

Agreement, shall provide the Agency of the other Contracting State with such evidence and other information in its possession as may be required to complete action on the claim.
3) The Agency of a Contracting State which receives a claim that was first filed with an Agency of the other Contracting State, shall without delay provide the Agency of the other Contracting State with such evidence and other available information in its possession as may be required for it to complete action on the claim.
4) The Agency of the Contracting State with which a claim for Benefits has been filed shall verify the information pertaining to the applicant and the applicant's family members. The Liaison Agencies of both Contracting States shall decide upon the types of information to be verified.
5) Upon request, the Agency of one Contracting State shall inform the Agency of the other Contracting State on bilingual forms of its decision to award or deny a claim filed under Part III of the Agreement.

Chapter IV. Miscellaneous Provisions

Article 5

In accordance with measures to be decided upon pursuant to paragraph 2 of Article 2 of this Administrative Arrangement, the Agency of one Contracting State shall, upon request by the Agency of the other Contracting State, furnish available information relating to the claim of any specified individual for the purpose of administering the Agreement.

For the purpose of facilitation of the implementation of the Agreement and this Administrative Arrangement, the Liaison Agencies may decide on measures for the provision and transmission of the electronic exchange of data.

Article 6

The Liaison Agencies shall exchange statistics on the number of certificates issued under Article 3 of this Administrative Arrangement and on the payments made to beneficiaries under the Agreement. These statistics shall be furnished annually in a manner to be decided upon by the Liaison Agencies.

Article 7
1) Where administrative assistance is requested and provided under Article 9 of the Agreement, expenses other than regular personnel and operating costs of the Agency providing the assistance shall be reimbursed, except as may be otherwise agreed to by the Competent Authorities or Liaison Agencies of the Contracting States.
2) Upon request, the Agency of either Contracting State shall furnish without cost to the Agency of the other Contracting State any medical information and documentation in its possession relevant to the disability of the claimant or beneficiary.
3) Where the Agency of a Contracting State requires that a person in the territory of the other Contracting State who is receiving or applying for Benefits under the Agreement submit to a medical examination, such examination, if requested by that Agency, shall be arranged by the Agency of the other Contracting State in accordance with the rules of the Agency making the arrangements and at the expense of the Agency requesting the examination.
4) The Agency of one Contracting State shall reimburse amounts owed under paragraphs 1 or 3 of this Article upon presentation of a statement of expenses by the Agency of the other Contracting State.

Article 8

The Agency shall pay Benefits directly to the beneficiary or his or her designee.

Upon request of the Agency referred to in paragraph 1 of this Article, a beneficiary shall submit proof, annually at minimum, that he or she is still alive.

Article 9

The Competent Authorities shall notify each other, in writing, of changes in the names of the Liaison Agencies without the need to modify the Administrative Arrangement.

Article 10

This Administrative Arrangement shall enter into force on the date of entry into force of the Agreement and remain in force so long as the Agreement is in force.

DONE at Ljubljana, this 17th day of January, 2017, in duplicate in the English and Slovenian languages, both texts being equally authentic.

For the United States of America: Brent R. Hartley

For the Republic of Slovenia: Anja Kopač Mrak

SOCIAL SECURITY MEMORANDUM

Date: November 21, 2017
Refer To: TCC
To: Stephen C. Goss, ASA, MAAA
Chief Actuary
From: Chris Chaplain, ASA /s/
Supervisory Actuary
Nettie Barrick /s/
Actuary

Subject: Estimated Effects of a Potential Totalization Agreement between Slovenia and the United States--information

This memorandum and the attached tables present estimates of the effects of implementing a potential totalization agreement with Slovenia assuming an effective date of January 1, 2019.

Table I shows the estimated net additional program costs to the Social Security systems of the United States (OASDI) and Slovenia under the potential agreement for fiscal years 2019 through 2026. In each case, these net additional program costs arise under the respective systems due to: (1) benefits payable because of the agreement; and (2) tax contributions eliminated for temporary foreign workers under the agreement.

The first three rows of Table 2 show estimates or the numbers of persons (as of mid-year) who would receive "totalized" benefits from each system. The fourth row of the table shows the number of Slovenian citizens living outside the U.S., and Slovenian residents who are citizens of a third country, who would be affected by removing the 5-year U.S. residency requirement for survivor or dependent benefits. The last two rows of the table show estimates of the numbers of temporary foreign workers in the respective com1tries who would be exempt from taxation by the local Social Security system under a totalization agreement. Under the agreement, U.S. workers working for a U.S. firm in Slovenia for a period expected to last 5 years or less would pay Social Security taxes only to the United States. Slovenian workers working for a Slovenian firm in the U.S. for a period expected to last 5 years or less would pay Social Security taxes only to the Slovenian system. We base estimates shown in the tables on the intermediate set of assumptions of the 2017 OASDI Trustees Report. The exchange rate used in these estimates is 0.850412 euros per U.S. dollar (1 EUR = $1.1759), the exchange rate as of October 17, 2017. To provide a frame of reference, the average exchange rate over the past 5 years is about 0.8370 EUR per U.S. dollar, with a low of about 0.7167 EUR per U.S. dollar and a high of about 0.9649 EUR per U.S. dollar.

These estimates are subject to much uncertainty. Many of the estimates are based on limited data for Slovenia and the assumption that certain relationships that apply on average for other countries where totalization agreements already exist will apply for Slovenia as well.

Numbers of Totalized Beneficiaries

To estimate the numbers of totalized beneficiaries under the U.S. Social Security system resulting from an agreement with Slovenia, we use two data sources for 21 of the existing agreement countries in a regression analysis.[105] From Census Bureau files, we estimate immigration and emigration. From counts of nonimmigrant visas issued by U.S. Foreign Service posts in each country to persons traveling to the U.S., over a 5-year period roughly 30 years ago when 2019-2026 retirees potentially receiving benefits under the totalization agreement were in their prime working years, we estimate the influx of temporary workers. This analysis yields an estimate of about 210 totalized beneficiaries under the U.S. Social Security system at the end of the 5th year of the potential agreement with Slovenia. For 9 of these existing-agreement countries, the predicted number of beneficiaries from the regression is higher than the actual number at the end of 5 years, by a median value of about 89 percent of the actual number. For 12 of these existing-agreement countries, the predicted number of beneficiaries from the regression is lower than the actual number, by a median value of about 29 percent of the actual number. Therefore, the number of OASDI beneficiaries at the end of the 5th year of implementation would be: (1) about 110, if the median relationship for countries with fewer beneficiaries than predicted by the regression analysis applies to Slovenia; and (2) about 290, if the median relationship for countries with more beneficiaries than predicted by the regression applies to Slovenia. To estimate the number of totalized Slovenian beneficiaries under the agreement, we use Census Bureau immigration data to make an initial estimate of the number of beneficiaries who will receive totalized

---

[105] We excluded 5 totalization agreement countries from the analysis -the Slovak Republic and Hungary because the agreements have *not* been in effect long enough for us to have five full years of data available, South Korea because work before 1986 in South Korea would not be counted as coverage in determining eligibility for totalized benefits, Luxembourg because of lack of data., and Canada because it is *a* border country with emigrant and immigrant patterns that would likely vary widely from those of Slovenia.

benefits under the Slovenian system. We then adjust this estimate based on a comparison of the number of beneficiaries under the U.S. system estimated using the same data, and the regression estimate for the U.S. system described in the previous paragraph.

Totalization agreements provide OASDI benefits mainly to three groups. The first group is Slovenian non-immigrants (temporary visa holders) who work in the U.S. for less than 10 years. These workers would have coverage under the U.S. Social Security system (unless they work for a Slovenian firm in the U.S. for 5 years or less after a totalization agreement becomes effective), and may be eligible for U.S. totalized benefits when their work in Slovenia is also considered. The second group is legal immigrants (generally permanent) from Slovenia to the U.S. who work in the U.S. for less than 10 years, frequently because they immigrate later in their working careers. The third group is emigrants from the U.S. to Slovenia (Slovenia-born or U.S.-born) who worked in the U.S. for less than 10 years, frequently because they emigrated relatively early in their careers. A totalization agreement between Slovenia and the United States precludes OASDI disability benefits for Slovenian workers employed by a Slovenian employer in the U.S. for 5 years or less who become disabled while working in the U.S. or shortly thereafter. However, temporary workers from Slovenia are unlikely to work long enough to qualify for U.S. disability benefits (generally at least 5 years), and are expected to be relatively healthy at the time they come to the U.S. to work. Therefore, we believe that reductions in OASDI disability benefits due to eliminating double taxation under a totalization agreement between Slovenia and the United States would be minimal. Similarly, we believe the reductions in disability benefits under the Slovenian system would be very small, relative to removing taxation to the Slovenian system for temporary U.S. workers in Slovenia.

5-Year Residency Requirement

In addition to estimates of the number of persons who would receive totalized OASDI benefits, we also estimate the number of alien dependents and survivors who do not meet the 5-year U.S. residency requirement for receipt of Social Security benefits. These individuals would receive OASDI benefits under a totalization agreement because the residency requirement does not apply to the potential Slovenian agreement.

Effects Related to Other US. Social Insurance Programs

The principal financial effects of a totalization agreement apply to the Social Security programs of the countries involved. Totalization agreements do not cover Medicare benefits. Thus, the U.S. cannot use credits for work in Slovenia to establish entitlement under the Medicare program. However, the tax side of the U.S. Medicare program would be affected because of the removal of double taxation for Slovenian workers who temporarily work in the U.S. for a Slovenian firm. We do not expect corresponding reduced Medicare outlays, because attainment of Medicare entitlement by these workers is highly unlikely under the current (no totalization) rules. Medicare eligibility is largely restricted to individuals who either: (1) are at least age 65 and eligible for U.S. Social Security benefits; or (2) were entitled to U.S. Social Security disability benefits (as a disabled worker, disabled widow(er), or disabled adult child) for at least 24 months. Furthermore, Medicare reimbursement is generally restricted to services provided in the U.S. Under the current (no totalization) rules, it is unlikely that temporary workers from Slovenia would (a) work enough to qualify for Medicare and (b) live in the U.S. when they might avail themselves of Medicare services; therefore, we believe a totalization agreement between Slovenia and the United States would reduce Medicare benefits very minimally. By law, totalization agreements do not affect payroll taxes paid for work injury (workers' compensation) and unemployment programs administered by the United States. Therefore, Slovenian temporary workers employed by Slovenian firms in the U.S., and their employers would still be required to pay any applicable workers' compensation and unemployment payroll taxes. These programs generally operate at the state, and not the federal, level.

Effects Related to Other Slovenian Social Insurance Programs

Under a totalization agreement, the Slovenian system would no longer require U.S. temporary workers in Slovenia (and their U.S.-based employers) to pay into Slovenia's national health and sickness insurance system. The reduction in contributions increases from an estimated $0.8 million in fiscal year (FY) 2019 to $1.5 million in FY 2026. These estimates assume the current contribution rate of 12.92% (6.56% employer, 6.36% employee) to the Slovenian national health insurance and sickness system continues through this period. By eliminating contributions to the Slovenian national health insurance and sickness system for these temporary U.S. workers in Slovenia, a totalization agreement would result in these workers no longer being eligible for services under that system. These foregone health insurance and sickness services represent a savings to the Slovenian system. The value of foregone national *health insurance and sickness* services for U.S. temporary workers in Slovenia is extremely difficult to estimate, but is expected to be small. It is very likely that U.S. temporary workers in Slovenia are relatively healthy and do not need much in the way of health services. Due to the assumed healthiness of the U.S. temporary worker population, the propensity to use health providers outside the Slovenian system, and the benefits paid by U.S. employers, we estimate, very roughly, that the value of benefits currently provided to U.S. workers by the Slovenian national health insurance and sickness system is about one-tenth of the amount of their contributions to that system. Table 1 shows the estimates of net costs to the Slovenian health insurance and sickness system, which range from $0.7 million in FY 2019 to $1.3 million in FY 2026-about 8 times the estimated net cost to the U.S. Medicare system for those years. Under a totalization agreement, the Slovenian system would lose work injury payroll tax contributions from the employers of affected workers. Also, the Slovenian system would lose maternity and unemployment payroll tax contributions from the affected workers and their employers. Under a totalization agreement, U.S. employers and their U.S. employees working temporarily in Slovenia would no longer contribute to these programs, and the Slovenian government would no longer pay benefits to these workers. We believe that most U.S. employers provide benefits to their employees, such that these workers would rarely receive Slovenian maternity benefits. Most U.S. employers also continue to pay earnings to people incapacitated due to injury for relatively short periods, such that Slovenia rarely pays work injury benefits to these workers. Therefore, we estimate that the value of Slovenian *work injury* benefits no longer paid to U.S. temporary workers affected by a potential totalization agreement would be very small. The Slovenian unemployment program pays benefits for a period of 3 to 19 months depending on the individual's number of years of contributions and age. However, we believe that very few temporary U.S. workers (working for U.S. employers) in Slovenia lose their jobs, and the few that do lose their jobs most likely move back to the United States and do not look for other work in Slovenia. Under a potential totalization agreement, U.S. temporary workers in Slovenia would no longer be eligible for Slovenian unemployment benefits. Because payment of unemployment benefits to temporary U.S. workers in Slovenia is unlikely, we expect the value of *unemployment* benefits no longer paid by Slovenia's system, under a totalization agreement, to be very small.

Long Range Financial Effects

Table 1. Estimated net additional program costs for the U.S. and Slovenian Social Security (and other) systems under a potential totalization agreement between the two countries, fiscal years 2019-2026 (in Millions)

	Fiscal year								
	2019	2020	2021	2022	2023	2024	2025	2026	Total, FY 2019-26
Financial Effects for the U.S.									
Social Security system:									
Increase in OASDI benefit payments	a	a	a	a	a	S1	$1	$1	$3
Reduction in OASDI tax contributions	a	a	a	$1	$1	1	1	1	4
Net OASDI cost	a	$1	$1	1	1	1	1	1	7
Net cost to the Medicare system	a	a	a	a	a	a	a	a	1
Net costs to the Social Security System of Slovenia:									
Increase in benefit payments	a	1	1	2	3	3	4	4	18
Reduction in OASDI tax contributions	$1	2	2	2	2	3	3	3	19
Total	2	3	3	4	5c	6	6	7	36
Net cost to the Slovenian national health insurance system[b]	1	1	1	1	1	1	1	1	9
Net cost for other Slovenian payroll tax contributions[c]	a	a	a	a	a	a	a	a	1

[a] Less than $500,000.
[b] Includes health insurance payroll tax contributions that the totalization agreement with Slovenia ould eliminate.
[c] Includes maternity, work injury, and unemployment payroll tax contributions that the totalization agreement with Slovenia would eliminate.

Notes:
1. The agreement is assumed to become effective on January 1, 2019.
2. The estimates are based on the intermediate assumptions of the 2017 Trustees Report.
3. Totals may not equal the sums of the components due to rounding.
4. Estimates are in U.S. dollars. The assumed exchange rate is 0.850412 euros per U.S. dollar.

Social Security Administration
Office of the Chief Actuary, November 21, 2017

Table 2. Estimated number of persons affected by a potential totalization agreement between the for the United States and Slovenia, fiscal years 2019-2026 (in thousands)

	2019	2020	2021	2022	2023	2024	2025	2026
Number of persons receiving a totalized OASDI benefit based in part on employment in Slovenia (in current-pay status at mid-year)	a	a	.1	.1	.2	.2	.2	.3
Number of persons receiving a totalized Slovenian benefit based in part on employment in the United States (in current-pay status at mid-year)	a	.2	.4	.6	.8	.9	1.0	1.1
Number of persons receiving both a totalized OASDI benefit and a totalized benefit from Slovenia (in current-pay status at mid-year).	a	a	a	a	a	a	a	.1
Number of residents of Slovenia, or Slovenian citizens living outside the U.S., who would now be able to receive OASDI dependent or survivor benefits because the 5-year residency requirement would no longer apply (in current-pay status at mid-year).	a	a	a	a	a	a	a	a
Number of U.S. employees in Slovenia who, along with their employers, would no longer make tax contributions during the year to the Social Security system of Slovenia	.1	.1	.1	.1	.1	.1	.1	.1
Number of Slovenian employees in the U.S who, along with their employers, would no longer make tax contributions during the year to the OASDHI trust funds	a	a	a	.1	.1	.1	.1	.1

[a] Fewer than 50.

Notes:
1. The agreement is assumed to become effective on January 1, 2019.
2. The estimates are based on the intermediate assumptions of the 2017 Trustees Report.

Social Security Administration
Office of the Chief Actuary
November 21, 2017

Table 3. Projected Net OASDI Cost of Implementing Proposed Totalization Agreement between U.S. and Slovenia

	Additional OASDI Net Benefits	Change in OASDI Payroll Taxes	Additional OASDI Net Cost	Additional OASDI Net Cost	Cumulative Additional OASDI
Year	For Year 1/	For Year	For Year 2/	For Year 2/	Net Cost 2/
	(Millions of CPI-Indexed 2017$)			(Millions of $, Present Value as of 1-1-17)	
2017	0	0	0	0	0
2018	0	0	0	0	0
2019	0	0	1	0	0
2020	0	0	1	1	1
2021	0	0	1	1	2
2022	0	0	1	1	3
2023	0	0	1	1	3
2024	0	0	1	1	4
2025	1	0	1	1	5
2026	1	-1	1	1	6
2027	1	-1	1	1	7
2028	1	-1	1	1	8
2029	1	-1	1	1	9
2030	1	-1	1	1	10
2031	1	-1	1	1	11
2032	1	-1	1	1	12
2033	1	-1	1	1	13
2034	1	-1	1	1	14
2035	1	-1	1	1	15
2036	1	-1	1	1	16
2037	1	-1	1	1	17
2038	1	-1	1	1	18
2039	1	-1	1	1	19
2040	1	-1	1	1	20
2041	1	-1	1	1	21
2042	1	-1	1	1	22
2043	1	-1	1	1	23
2044	1	-1	1	1	23
2045	1	-1	1	1	24

Table 3. (Continued)

Year	Additional OASDI Net Benefits For Year 1/	Change in OASDI Payroll Taxes For Year	Additional OASDI Net Cost For Year 2/	Additional OASDI Net Cost For Year 2/	Cumulative Additional OASDI Net Cost 2/
	(Millions of CPI-Indexed 2017$)			(Millions of $, Present Value as of 1-1-17)	
2046	1	-1	2	1	25
2047	1	-1	2	1	26
2048	1	-1	2	1	27
2049	1	-1	2	1	28
2050	1	-1	2	1	29
2051	1	-1	2	1	29
2052	1	-1	2	1	30
2053	1	-1	2	1	31
2054	1	-1	2	1	32
2055	1	-1	2	1	33
2056	1	-1	2	1	33
2057	1	-1	2	1	34
2058	1	-1	2	1	35
2059	1	-1	2	1	36
2060	1	-1	2	1	36
2061	1	-1	2	1	37
2062	1	-1	2	1	38
2063	1	-1	2	1	39
2064	1	-1	2	1	39
2065	1	-1	2	1	40
2066	1	-1	2	1	41
2067	1	-1	2	1	41
2068	1	-1	2	1	42
2069	1	-1	2	1	43
2070	1	-1	2	1	44
2071	1	-1	2	1	44
2072	1	-1	2	1	45
2073	1	-1	2	1	46
2074	1	-1	2	1	46
2075	1	-1	2	1	47
2076	1	-1	3	1	48
2077	1	-1	3	1	48
2078	1	-1	3	1	49
2079	1	-1	3	1	49
2080	1	-1	3	1	50

Agreement on Social Security between the United States ... 211

Year	Additional OASDI Net Benefits For Year 1/	Change in OASDI Payroll Taxes For Year	Additional OASDI Net Cost For Year 2/	Additional OASDI Net Cost For Year 2/	Cumulative Additional OASDI Net Cost 2/
	(Millions of CPI-Indexed 2017$)			(Millions of $, Present Value as of 1-1-17)	
2081	2			-1	
2082	2			-1	
2033	2			-1	
2084	2	-1	3	1	53
2085	2	-1	3	1	53
2086	2	-1	3	1	54
2087	2	-1	3	1	54
2088	2	-1	3	1	55
2089	2	-1	3	1	55
2090	2	-1	3	1	56
2091	2	-1	3	1	57

Based on Intermediate Assumptions of the 2017 Trustees Report.
1/ Additional benefits less revenue to OASDI from taxes on benefits.
2/ Additional net benefit payments minus change in payroll-tax revenue.

Social Security Administration
Office of the Chief Actuary
November 21, 2017

Implementing the potential totalization agreement between the U.S. and Slovenia would decrease the long-range (75-year) actuarial balance of the OASDI program by an amount that is estimated to be negligible (that is, by less than 0.005 percent of taxable payroll).

Table 3 displays the components of the estimated net cost to the OASDI Trust Funds for years 2017 through 2091 on a "CPI-indexed to 2017" basis, i.e., indexing the amounts back to the year 2017 by assumed changes in the consumer price index (CPI). In addition, the table displays total estimated OASDI net costs on an annual and cumulative present-value basis, i.e., indexing the amounts back to January I, 2017 by projected interest rates earned by the OASDI Trust Funds on special-issue U.S. Government bonds.

INDEX

A

adjustment, 120, 161
aggregation, 79, 121
American Samoa, 7, 106, 147
authentication, 82, 127, 167, 192
authenticity, 127, 167
authorities, 23, 47, 80, 82, 123, 127, 164, 167, 190, 192
average earnings, 19, 44, 78, 118, 119, 158, 159, 160, 187

B

Banco de Previsión Social (Social Security Bank), 71, 73, 87, 88, 107, 109, 134, 135
beneficiaries, 11, 20, 22, 35, 40, 55, 58, 59, 73, 90, 92, 93, 110, 120, 137, 151, 160, 161, 178, 183, 199, 202
benefit eligibility, 3, 8, 11, 12, 18, 21, 29, 102, 108, 110, 111, 116, 121, 131, 143, 148, 151, 152, 156, 157, 163, 171
benefit protection, vii, 2, 70, 142
benefits, 3, 4, 5, 8, 9, 11, 12, 18, 19, 20, 21, 22, 23, 26, 27, 28, 29, 30, 34, 36, 38, 40, 44, 45, 49, 51, 54, 55, 57, 58, 59, 60, 61, 62, 64, 67, 72, 73, 92, 93, 94, 95, 96, 98, 101, 102, 108, 109, 110, 111, 120, 121, 143, 149, 150, 152, 159, 163, 182, 201, 202, 203, 204, 205, 206, 208, 211
bilateral, vii, 2, 11, 70, 110, 121, 142, 150, 151
bonds, 67, 101, 211

C

Caja de Jubilaciones y Pensiones Bancarias (Banking Pension and Retirement Fund), 72, 73, 107, 110
Caja Notarial de Seguridad. Social (Notarial Social Security Fund), 71, 73, 107, 109
census, 58, 59, 93, 202
certificate, 6, 33, 53, 54, 88, 105, 135, 146, 175, 176, 197
certification, 26, 48, 82, 127, 167, 192
child benefit, 10
children, 10, 106, 120, 160, 161
Chile, vii, 2, 70, 142
citizens, 5, 7, 12, 14, 15, 22, 57, 64, 92, 98, 106, 111, 113, 114, 152, 154, 155, 201, 208

citizenship, 7, 9, 22, 38, 72, 106, 108, 147, 149, 182
citizenship of the Republic of Slovenia Act, 147, 181
compensation, 61, 95, 205
competent authorities, 1, 2, 17, 23, 24, 26, 28, 31, 36, 37, 43, 46, 47, 49, 50, 52, 55, 56, 69, 77, 80, 81, 83, 85, 87, 90, 115, 123, 124, 127, 128, 130, 133, 138, 156, 164, 165, 167, 168, 170, 176, 179, 180, 186, 190, 192, 194, 197, 199, 200
competent institutions, 72, 82, 83, 90, 108, 123, 125, 127, 128, 129, 130, 131, 138
compliance, 86, 132
confidentiality, 24, 25, 35, 47, 48, 81, 82, 124, 126, 137, 165, 166, 178, 190, 191
conformity, 31, 52, 87, 133, 174, 195
consumer price index, 20, 67, 101, 161, 211
cost, 2, 20, 36, 55, 63, 67, 70, 90, 96, 97, 101, 120, 138, 142, 161, 179, 199, 206, 207, 211
cost of living, 20, 120, 161
CPI, 65, 66, 67, 99, 100, 101, 209, 210, 211
CPT, 67
currency, 28, 50, 84, 130, 170, 193

D

defined benefit pension, 159
delegates, 107
denial, 177
deprivation, 147
destruction, 25, 125, 166
disability, 4, 5, 8, 9, 10, 20, 29, 36, 39, 55, 60, 61, 73, 90, 94, 95, 96, 97, 103, 104, 108, 109, 110, 119, 120, 123, 131, 138, 144, 145, 149, 150, 160, 161, 171, 179, 183, 199, 203, 204
disability benefit, 4, 5, 8, 20, 60, 61, 94, 95, 97, 103, 104, 144, 145, 203, 204

disclosure, 24, 25, 48, 82, 124, 126, 165, 166, 191
discrimination, 12, 111, 152
dual coverage, 3, 4, 6, 15, 17, 102, 105, 115, 143, 146, 156

E

early retirement, 160
earnings, 4, 8, 13, 18, 19, 20, 38, 62, 72, 108, 112, 116, 117, 118, 148, 153, 157, 158, 160, 182, 206
economic partners, vii, 2, 142
economic status, 9, 39, 72, 109, 149, 182
EEA, 151
emigration, 59, 93, 202
employees, 4, 15, 16, 20, 42, 62, 64, 76, 98, 103, 114, 115, 144, 155, 156, 159, 185, 206, 208
employers, 16, 20, 25, 43, 48, 61, 62, 64, 82, 95, 96, 98, 113, 126, 154, 159, 166, 191, 205, 206, 208
employment, 8, 13, 14, 15, 16, 29, 38, 41, 42, 43, 51, 64, 72, 74, 75, 76, 85, 98, 108, 112, 113, 115, 131, 148, 153, 154, 156, 161, 171, 182, 184, 185, 186, 194, 208
equality, 119, 159
European Union, 70, 151
examinations, 36, 90, 124, 138, 164, 179
exchange rate, 58, 63, 92, 97, 201, 207
exclusion, 10

F

family members, 14, 16, 34, 41, 54, 89, 115, 136, 155, 177, 198
Federal Republic of Yugoslavia, 152
fiscal year, 57, 63, 64, 91, 96, 97, 98, 201, 205, 207, 208
foreign nationals, 22, 107

Index

funds, 7, 8, 20, 108, 119, 148, 182

G

government revenues, 20, 119

H

health insurance, 9, 62, 96, 97, 110, 148, 150, 205, 207
health services, 96, 205
Hungary, 93, 202

I

immigrants, 59, 93, 203
immigration, 58, 59, 93, 202
Immigration and Nationality Act, 7, 37, 71, 106, 147, 181
immunity, 16
incarceration, 10
income, 10, 18, 20, 44, 78, 117, 119
indexing, 67, 101, 211
information exchange, 25, 126, 166
initiation, 85, 130
institutions, 104, 108, 148, 149, 182
integrity, 24, 25, 124, 126, 165, 166
interest rates, 67, 101, 211
Internal Revenue Service (IRS), 7, 14, 108, 113, 148, 154

J

Japan, vii, 2, 70, 142

K

Korea, vii, 2, 58, 70, 93, 142, 202

L

languages, 31, 52, 56, 86, 91, 133, 139, 173, 180, 195, 200
laws, 4, 5, 6, 7, 8, 9, 10, 11, 12, 13, 14, 15, 16, 17, 18, 19, 20, 21, 23, 24, 25, 26, 27, 28, 29, 32, 33, 34, 35, 37, 38, 39, 40, 41, 42, 43, 44, 45, 47, 48, 49, 50, 51, 53, 71, 73, 75, 104, 107, 109, 110, 113, 114, 124, 126, 128, 137, 145, 146, 147, 149, 150, 151, 153, 155, 165, 166, 169, 178, 181, 183, 185
laws and regulations, 7, 37, 71, 107, 147, 151, 181, 183
legislation, 10, 11, 20, 39, 40, 73, 74, 110, 150, 151, 183
liaison agencies, 5, 23, 32, 34, 35, 36, 46, 53, 54, 55, 145, 149, 164, 174, 175, 176, 177, 178, 179, 180, 182, 189, 196, 197, 198, 199, 200
liaison institution, 72, 80, 84, 87, 88, 89, 90, 104, 105, 108, 123, 129, 134, 135, 136, 137, 138
lifetime, 19, 44, 78, 118, 158, 160, 187
loss of benefit rights, 4, 103, 144

M

Mandatory Pension Insurance Scheme, 8, 10, 22, 38, 39, 46
maritime transportation, 4, 103, 144
marriage, 29, 120, 131, 171
means tested, 20, 119
medical, 9, 36, 38, 55, 72, 90, 108, 124, 138, 149, 164, 179, 182, 199
Medicare, 9, 61, 63, 95, 96, 97, 109, 150, 204, 206, 207
Ministerio de Trabajo y Seguridad Social, 71, 107
Ministry of Welfare, 7, 37

N

nationality, 9, 12, 38, 72, 108, 111, 149, 152, 182
negotiation, 28, 130, 170
Norway, vii, 2, 70, 142

O

old age, 21, 45, 73, 109
operating costs, 35, 36, 55, 90, 137, 138, 178, 179, 199
Oriental Republic of Uruguay, 69, 70, 71, 86, 87, 91, 106, 133, 139
overlap, 78, 121
oversight, 20

P

parents, 20, 120, 147, 160, 161
payroll, 61, 62, 67, 95, 97, 101, 205, 206, 207, 211
pension, 7, 8, 10, 17, 19, 20, 21, 22, 38, 39, 43, 45, 46, 72, 73, 107, 110, 119, 146, 148, 150, 159, 160, 174, 175, 183, 196
period of coverage, 8, 38, 72, 108, 148, 182
permission, 12, 111, 152
permit, 5, 12, 112, 121, 131, 152, 171
personal data, 8, 9, 23, 24, 25, 35, 38, 47, 48, 72, 81, 82, 108, 109, 124, 125, 126, 137, 149, 164, 165, 166, 178, 182, 190, 191
personal relations, 9, 39, 72, 109, 149, 182
personal relationship, 9, 39, 72, 109, 149, 182
police, 108
population, 96, 205
price index, 161
principles, 5, 104, 145
professionals, 108

protection, vii, 2, 24, 25, 35, 47, 48, 70, 81, 82, 124, 126, 137, 142, 165, 166, 178, 190, 191

R

reciprocity, 30, 51
reform, 160
refugee status, 9, 38, 72, 108, 149, 182
regression, 58, 59, 92, 93, 202, 203
regression analysis, 58, 93, 202
regulations, 9, 10, 11, 19, 24, 39, 73, 74, 108, 109, 110, 118, 124, 150, 151, 158, 165, 183
rehabilitation, 160
reimburse, 36, 56, 90, 138, 179, 199
requirements, 3, 4, 5, 10, 11, 12, 18, 19, 21, 31, 44, 45, 52, 77, 82, 86, 102, 103, 104, 110, 111, 112, 116, 119, 120, 127, 132, 143, 144, 145, 151, 152, 156, 159, 161, 162, 167, 186, 188, 192
resolution, 85, 130
restrictions, 5, 12, 111, 112, 152
retirement, 4, 5, 10, 20, 72, 73, 79, 96, 97, 103, 104, 107, 110, 119, 120, 121, 144, 145, 160
retirement age, 160
revenue, 67, 101, 211
rights, 4, 11, 12, 24, 26, 27, 29, 30, 40, 49, 51, 74, 83, 86, 103, 111, 124, 128, 131, 132, 144, 151, 165, 168, 171, 173, 192, 194, 195
rules, 3, 4, 6, 17, 18, 19, 21, 33, 36, 56, 61, 79, 95, 102, 103, 104, 105, 108, 115, 116, 119, 121, 122, 135, 143, 144, 145, 146, 151, 156, 159, 175, 176, 179, 199, 204

Index

S

scope, 10, 11, 23, 47, 80, 110, 113, 119, 123, 151, 154, 164, 190
security, vii, 2, 4, 12, 13, 17, 70, 104, 105, 110, 111, 112, 142, 145, 146, 150, 152, 153
self employment, 72, 154
self-employed, 4, 8, 14, 15, 20, 33, 38, 42, 53, 74, 75, 88, 103, 105, 109, 110, 112, 113, 115, 119, 135, 144, 153, 154, 175, 184, 185, 197
self-employed person, 4, 15, 20, 33, 42, 53, 88, 103, 105, 109, 110, 113, 115, 119, 135, 144, 154, 175, 197
self-employment, 4, 8, 15, 18, 38, 42, 44, 74, 78, 85, 108, 112, 113, 117, 131, 148, 153, 154, 171, 182, 184, 185, 194
services, 61, 95, 96, 107, 108, 115, 119, 155, 204, 205
Servicio de Retiros y Pensiones Policiales (Police Retirement and Pension Fund), 72, 73, 107, 110
Social Insurance Administration, 5, 7, 32, 33, 38, 53, 54
social security, vii, 1, 2, 3, 5, 7, 8, 10, 11, 12, 13, 15, 16, 17, 19, 20, 21, 23, 26, 30, 38, 39, 43, 51, 62, 69, 70, 71, 102, 103, 104, 105, 106, 107, 108, 110, 111, 112, 115, 116, 119, 121, 123, 126, 127, 135, 141, 142, 143, 144, 145, 146, 147, 148, 149, 150, 151, 152, 153, 155, 156, 159, 164, 167, 175, 181, 183
Social Security Act, 1, 2, 3, 8, 9, 10, 21, 38, 39, 45, 69, 70, 73, 78, 102, 108, 109, 118, 141, 142, 143, 149, 150, 159, 183, 188
Social Security Administration, 2, 5, 6, 7, 32, 33, 38, 53, 54, 63, 64, 67, 70, 71, 87, 88, 97, 98, 101, 105, 107, 108, 134, 135, 142, 146, 148, 174, 175, 176, 182, 196, 197, 207, 209, 211
social security contributions, 4, 17, 43, 103, 144
social security coverage, vii, 2, 12, 13, 16, 21, 70, 111, 112, 115, 121, 135, 142, 152, 153, 155, 175
social security systems, vii, 2, 3, 70, 102, 121, 142, 143
social security totalization agreements, vii, 2, 70, 142
solidarity, 79, 121
South Korea, 58, 93, 202
statistics, 35, 55, 90, 120, 137, 178, 199
statutes, 23, 24, 25, 35, 47, 48, 81, 82, 124, 125, 126, 137, 164, 165, 166, 178, 190, 191
survivors, 4, 8, 9, 10, 12, 20, 39, 60, 73, 94, 97, 103, 104, 108, 109, 111, 112, 116, 119, 120, 144, 145, 149, 150, 151, 152, 157, 161, 183, 184, 204
Switzerland, vii, 2, 70, 142

T

taxation, vii, 2, 3, 13, 16, 58, 60, 61, 70, 92, 94, 95, 102, 112, 142, 143, 153, 201, 203, 204
taxes, 13, 58, 61, 67, 92, 95, 96, 101, 109, 112, 153, 201, 205, 211
TCC, 57, 91, 200
territory, 12, 13, 14, 15, 16, 17, 22, 29, 36, 40, 41, 42, 43, 46, 51, 55, 74, 75, 76, 85, 90, 106, 111, 112, 113, 114, 115, 131, 138, 147, 152, 153, 154, 155, 156, 163, 171, 179, 184, 185, 186, 189, 194, 199
Title I, 9, 39, 73, 109, 150, 183
Title II, 9, 39, 73, 109, 150, 183
translation, 82, 127
transmission, 24, 25, 35, 47, 55, 81, 124, 125, 165, 166, 178, 190, 198

transportation, 4, 15, 42, 76, 103, 114, 144, 155, 185
treaties, 10, 11, 39, 73, 110, 150, 183
treatment, 12, 40, 74, 111, 119, 152, 159, 184
trust fund, 98, 208, 67, 101, 211
Tryggingastofnun rikisins, 7, 32, 33, 54

U

U.S. Social Security Administration, 6
unemployment insurance, 150
unforeseen circumstances, 17, 156
uninsured, 8, 9, 108, 109, 149, 150

V

Velferdarraduneytid, 7

W

wage level, 161
wages, 18, 44, 78, 117, 161
White House, 2, 70, 142
work activity, 15, 17, 112, 120, 153
workers, vii, 2, 4, 6, 10, 14, 17, 57, 58, 59, 60, 61, 62, 70, 92, 93, 94, 95, 96, 103, 105, 108, 113, 115, 119, 120, 142, 144, 146, 148, 153, 154, 156, 159, 160, 201, 202, 203, 204, 205, 206

Social Security: Benefits, Changes and Proposals

Editor: Jonathon Ibarra

Series: Government Procedures and Operations

Book Description: The CRS reports included in this book provide an overview of Social Security financing and benefits under current law. It also covers how the Social Security program is financed and how the Social Security trust funds work.

Softcover ISBN: 978-1-53614-153-5
Retail Price: $82

Social Security and Retirement Benefits: Programs, Perspectives and Future Directions

Editor: Allison Clark

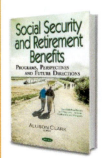

Series: Social Welfare Policies and Programs – Patterns, Implications and Prospects

Book Description: This book provides new research on Social Security programs and retirement benefits, reviews different perspectives and the programs' future directions.

Softcover ISBN: 978-1-53610-474-5
Retail Price: $82

Policy Options and Long-Term Projections for Social Security

Editor: Juanita Harmon

Series: Retirement Issues, Plans and Lifestyles

Book Description: This book considers 36 policy options that are among those commonly proposed by policymakers and analysts as a means of restoring financial security to the Social Security program. Furthermore, this book presents additional information about CBO's long-term projections for Social Security in the form of 15 exhibits that illustrate the program's finances and the distribution of benefits paid to and payroll taxes collected from various groups of people.

Hardcover ISBN: 978-1-63485-443-6
Retail Price: $150

The Future of Social Security: Goals, Outlook, Options

Editor: William L. Harmon

Series: Retirement Issues, Plans and Lifestyles

Book Description: This book is intended to describe, in a concise and easy-to-understand way, the complexities of Social Security, the challenges the programs face, and the options available to address these challenges.

Softcover ISBN: 978-1-63485-191-6
Retail Price: $95